Orphan Song

Orphan Song

Sean Dixon

Orphan Song
first published 2022 by Scirocco Drama
An imprint of J. Gordon Shillingford Publishing Inc.

Scirocco Drama Editor: Glenda MacFarlane
Cover design by Doowah Design
Author photo by SD Photography
Production photos by Cylla von Tiedemann

Printed and bound in Canada on 100% post-consumer recycled paper.
We acknowledge the financial support of the Manitoba Arts Council and The Canada Council for the Arts for our publishing program.

Production inquiries to:
seanmorleydixon@gmail.com

Library and Archives Canada Cataloguing in Publication

Title: Orphan song / Sean Dixon.
Names: Dixon, Sean, 1964- author.
Identifiers: Canadiana 20220429839 | ISBN 9781990737176 (softcover)
Subjects: LCGFT: Drama.
Classification: LCC PS8557.I97 O77 2022 | DDC C812/.54—dc23

J. Gordon Shillingford Publishing
P.O. Box 86, RPO Corydon Avenue, Winnipeg, MB Canada R3M 3S3

For Ava

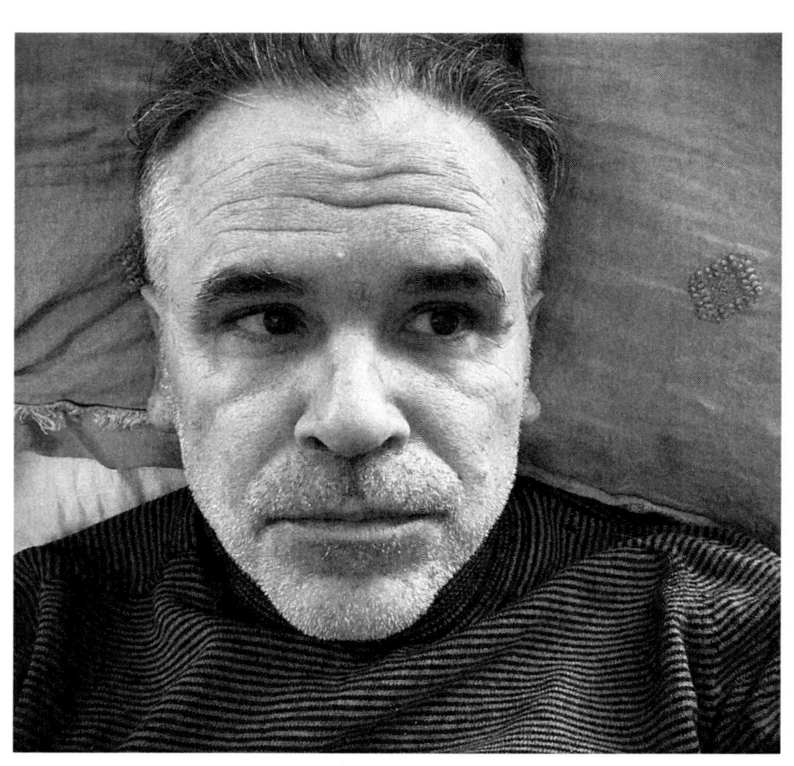

Sean Dixon

Sean Dixon is a playwright best known for his work with Victoria's Theatre SKAM and Winnipeg's renowned Primus Theatre. He's written several shows for the Okanagan's Caravan Farm Theatre and Eastern Ontario's Blyth Festival, and will be publishing a novel next year with Calgary's Freehand Books. In 2014, he was nominated for the Governor General's Award for his play *A God in Need of Help*, first produced at Toronto's Tarragon Theatre.

Other works include the plays *The Wilberforce Hotel, The Orange Dot, Jumbo, The Child Empress, France, (or, 'The Niqab'), Falling Back Home, The Painting, Sam's Last Dance, Billy Nothin'*, and *The Gift of the Coat*; the novels *The Many Revenges of Kip Flynn* and *The Girls Who Saw Everything*, and a picture book (with illustrator Lily Snowden-Fine), *The Family Tree.*

Sean lives with his wife, the multi-award-winning documentary maker Katerina Cizek, and a ten-year-old daughter whose brilliant, funny, stubborn character inspires much of his current work.

Acknowledgements

Thanks to Frank Donato, Richard Rose, Mike Payette, Andrea Vagianos, Cameron Johnston, Gerry Egan, Natasha Parsons, Kait Morrow, Susana Bejar, Maddie Bautista, Joanna Falck, Eva Barrie, Esther Jun, Audrey Dwyer, Courtney Ch'ng Lancaster, Rachel Cairns, Paul Hopkins, Maggie Huculak, Alden Adair, Khadijah Roberts-Abdullah, Janet Laine Green, Maria Vacratsis, Susanna Fournier, Amiel Gladstone, Brendan Wall, Kaitlyn Riordan, Phoebe Hu, Alix Sideris, Vicki Stroich, Amiel Gladstone, Chala Hunter, Greg Gale, Lucy Hill, Andrea Lee Norwood, Charlin McIsaac.

Playwright's Note

I don't see this play as a story about the eponymous "last Neanderthal." It has long been established that early modern humans shared the earth with their Neanderthal counterparts for tens of thousands of years. This is a story of one crisis that happened along the way—a crisis for a desperate community of Neanderthals who were bewildered by their own suffering, that transformed into a mixing of two small communities into one.

Our genetic history tells us that such mixings happened several times during our shared history.

Up until very recently we believed that Neanderthals were a brutish throwback to an earlier species in our evolutionary line that, through a strange bit of happenstance, lived alongside our early modern human forebears for tens of thousands of years.

In the 19th century, archeologists found Neanderthal remains that looked stooped and misshapen, and so they surmised that Neanderthals were apelike and ugly and ignorant.

A decade or so ago, however, scientists miraculously managed to isolate a complete Neanderthal genome.

With that came a startling discovery: every single modern human possesses somewhere between 2 and 5 percent Neanderthal DNA—and not the same DNA either: among the population of the human race, there exists up to 25 percent of the Neanderthal genome, in total.

Turns out they are not our forebears, after all. They are our siblings and ourselves.

What's more, we have discovered compelling evidence of a vibrant culture: wall drawings, strange powders that may have been used for medical or cosmetic purposes; garment design that featured feathers; even an ability to make fire, which skill had been denied them in such famous stories as the 1981 film, *Quest for Fire*.

Analysis of throat bones have concluded that Neanderthals could speak. Vocal experts have speculated that they might have spoken in higher pitches than Early Modern Humans, leading one prehistory professor, Steven Mithen, to imagine that they may have taken a whole different approach to language than the rest of us, that perhaps they had been inspired by birdsong.

As Mo says in the play, "Maybe we all learned our speech that way: through mimicry and then longing."

As for the early find of the stooped, misshapen Neanderthal remains: it became clear that this was the skeleton of an elderly man who had lived through several traumas in his life, and that, due to the love and care of his community, his wounds had healed, and he had lived to a relatively ripe old age.

So, instead of being evidence of Neanderthals' gracelessness and ignorance, the scars on that old skeleton were rather a testament to their compassion, their foresight, their love, their medical abilities, their human priorities, their care for one another.

+

All discussions of theme aside, however, here is what I hope playwrights will take away from reading this play:

I set out in the first draft to describe the action of this play via a myriad of stage directions.

Director Richard Rose conducted a workshop and, since the play came off as little more than a recitation of action, the reading fell flat.

At the end of the workshop day, he related a story of having done another play in which they spent the entire rehearsal period trying to live up to the beautifully described stage directions.

They were unable to do it, it bogged them down. The play did not succeed.

His only note, then, was to suggest that I cut my stage directions entirely and convey what I needed using spoken text alone.

"But there are animals in this play," I protested. "But the Neanderthal characters whistle like birds."

"Aren't you a musician?" he responded. "Can't you compose little scores for the Neanderthals?"

Reader, my musical ability is this: I am a banjo player.

When I sat down with the text after that, I had to figure out how to convey a traumatized child who would not sit still, with sounds alone. I had to convey a bear attack, a rejected flirtation, the shunning of one group of people by another, using nothing more than the sounds they made, written down.

I worried that nuances would be lost, moments of behaviour that I had imagined would disappear.

Well, and it's true: physical bits I had imagined were lost, despite my efforts to vocalize my way through them. It was important for me to imagine them, of course, so that I could vocalize my way through them and then write those vocalizations down. But they were replaced—and undoubtedly improved upon—by bits that were created entirely by the actors in consultation with the director, seeking only to interpret the text and follow the feeling.

So, to look at it from an actor's point of view: when a character laughs hysterically and then screams and then another character says ouch, you can easily convey the chaos and violence of that in a table read, with your voice alone. And then, when you get on your feet, you are free to convey it onstage however you wish, your only priority being to live up to the force of the sounds you made and the logic of where they lead.

There is freedom in that for the actor. It demands physicality, but not a prescribed physicality.

The text is a score.

If you, playwright, prioritize physicality, then make your text a score, not a description. That's what I hope playwrights will take away from reading this play.

Within reason, of course. There's no need to make it a puzzle. I restored stage directions here and there. The English spoken in this play is derived from a 200-word linguistic tool called the Swadesh List, a vocabulary about equivalent to the communication skills of a raccoon. It doesn't quite convey enough in terms of communication. So I needed to restore a gesture here and there: the cupping of blood in a palm, the dressing of a child or a wound.

But a friend of mine came to the closing performance and asked if the script was like a shooting script for a film. That's what it looked like to him. But it's nothing like a shooting script for a film. In the text-based approach to theatre that we prioritize in the English-speaking world, this kind of vocal scoring — I submit — is how to promote a physical approach.

I began my career in the physical theatre, first acting in and then writing text for Primus Theatre in Winnipeg. To me, there was always a gulf between the text of those plays and their physicality. I've always wanted to bridge that gulf. The text for *Orphan Song* is the closest I've come to fulfilling that ambition.

Sean Dixon

2022

Production History

Orphan Song was first programmed in Tarragon Theatre's 2019/20 season, under the artistic directorship of Richard Rose. The production was delayed due to COVID-19 and was reprogrammed as part of the 2021/22 season, under the artistic directorship of Mike Payette. It opened on April 1, 2022 and ran until April 24th, 2022, with the following cast and creative team:

Cast

Heather Marie Annis: .... Neanderthals/Carrion Bird Body/Good People/Young Neanderthal Woman/Mammoth/Blackbirds/Hyena

Beau Dixon: .... Gorse

Philippa Domville: .... Swing - Chorus

Sophie Goulet: .... Mo

Phoebe Hu: .... Neanderthals/Dog/Rabbit/Mammoth/Blackbirds/ Hyena 3/Carrion Bird Body 2/Music & Puppet Captain

Germaine Konji: .... Neanderthals/Good People Woman/Hedgehog 2/Mammoth/Blackbirds

Ahmed Moneka: .... Neanderthals/Carrion Bird Wing/Good People Man 2/Toad/Mammoth/Blackbirds/Hyena 2/Another Hedgehog

Kaitlin Morrow: .... Child / Chicky - Puppet Master

Kaitlyn Riordan: .... Neanderthals / Good People / Hedgehog 1 / Mammoth / Blackbirds / Moon

Terry Tweed: .... Gran

Daniel Williston: .... Neanderthals / Carrion Bird Wing / Good People Man 1 / Bear / Mammoth / Blackbirds

Creative Team

Director: .... Richard Rose

Set Design: .... Graeme S. Thomson

Costume Design: .... Charlotte Dean

Music Direction and Sound Design: .... Juliet Palmer

Stage Manager: .... Sandy Plunkett

Apprentice Stage Manager: .... Alysse Szatkowski

Head Scenic Painter: .... Sara Ahmadieh

Scenic Paint Assistant: .... Sebastian Cox

Updated musical notation and transcription by Phoebe Hu.

The Neanderthals (Kaitlin Morrow, Daniel Williston, Phoebe Hu, Heather Marie Annis, Ahmed Moneka, Philippa Domville) sing their dying song. Photo by Cylla von Tiedemann.

Chicky's mother (Phoebe Hu) gives Chicky (Kaitlin Morrow) a healing salve in an acorn shell. Photo by Cylla von Tiedemann.

Gorse (Beau Dixon) and Mo (Sophie Goulet) bury their child Cal. Photo by Cylla von Tiedemann.

The Good People (Daniel Williston, Kaitlyn Riordan, Ahmed Moneka, Heather Marie Annis, Philippa Domville) drive Gorse and Mo away. Photo by Cylla von Tiedemann.

Gorse (Beau Dixon) hunts. Photo by Cylla von Tiedemann.

The young Neanderthal woman (Heather Marie Annis) goes into the water as Gran (Terry Tweed) calls to her. Photo by Cylla von Tiedemann.

A carrion bird (Daniel Williston, Heather Marie Annis, Ahmed Moneka) approaches. Photo by Cylla von Tiedemann.

Gran (Terry Tweed) cares for Mo (Sophie Goulet). Photo by Cylla von Tiedemann.

The mammoth (Phoebe Hu, Philippa Domville, Heather Marie Annis, Kaitlyn Riordan, Ahmed Moneka). Photo by Cylla von Tiedemann.

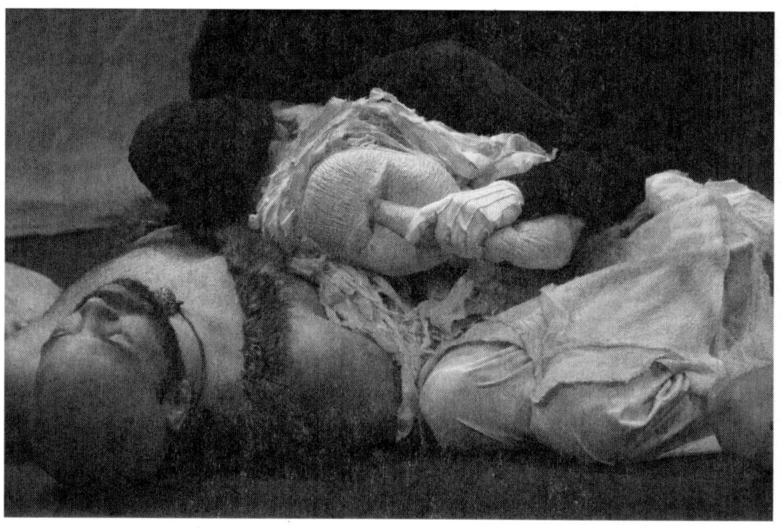

Chicky (Kaitlin Morrow) curls up against Gorse (Beau Dixon) to sleep. Photo by Cylla von Tiedemann.

Gorse (Beau Dixon) tries to communicate with the young Neanderthal woman (Heather Marie Annis) as Chicky (Kaitlin Morrow) clings to him and Gran (Terry Tweed) and the other Neanderthals (Daniel Williston, Phoebe Hu, Philippa Domville, Kaitlyn Riordan, Ahmed Moneka) look on. Photo by Cylla von Tiedemann.

Gorse (Beau Dixon), Mo (Sophie Goulet), Gran (Terry Tweed), Chicky (Kaitlin Morrow), and the young Neanderthal woman (Heather Marie Annis) form a new family. Photo by Cylla von Tiedemann.

Characters

Chicky: .... A female Neanderthal child

Gorse: .... An early modern human* adult male

Mo:....................................... An early modern human adult female

Gran:.................................... Gorse's mother

Moon: .... The moon

Neanderthal Woman:......... Who joins the family

Men and women of the Neanderthal people, carrion birds, men and women of the "Good People," a toad, a hedgehog, a rabbit, a mammoth, a bear, blackbirds, hyenas, another hedgehog.

* Formerly known as "Cro-Magnon"

Production Notes

A Note on the Early Modern Humans' Language:

The English spoken in the play by Gorse, Mo and the other Early Modern Humans is derived from a list of 200 words, considered basic to every language, known as the "Swadesh List." Several variations of this list exist. I took the liberty of allowing my characters a coinage or two, also added the words "piper" and "chick," and sounds for "yes" and "no" to my copy of the list, which is printed as an appendix at the end of the play. And somewhere along the line, my characters also started using the word "Why," which is not on the list.

The exception to this use of limited language is the act of prayer, or reflection, which assumes that thought transcends vocabulary.

A Note on the Neanderthal's Whistling Language:

Lines of musical notation have been provided as an approximate guide to relative tone and rhythm, not pitch. The performer should employ them as a springboard to their best birdlike communication.

Sound files are available upon request.

A Note on Numbers and Counting:

The Early Modern Human numerical system in this play is based on sets of five. (The Swadesh List doesn't provide any more numbers). So whereas we Late Modern Humans count to 10 and then "start over," in a manner of speaking, with 11, these Early Modern Humans end at the number five and then start over with one-one, one-two, one-three, one-four, one-five. Then they start over again with two-one, two-two, etc.

Gorse's habitual problem when counting sticks is that he often jumps straight to two-one after getting to five. It would be like a person counting to ten and then jumping straight to twenty-one. This may sound like I'm saying he's stupid, but I think it's more because he intuits the existence of zero and is confused by its absence, even though that is a concept that won't be established for another ten thousand years. I think he'd get it right if the system went like this—

> zero-one, zero-two, zero-three, zero-four, zero-five;
> one-one, one-two, one-three, one-four, one-five;
> two-one, two-two, etc.
>
> —but it doesn't. So Gorse often ends up saying,
>
> one, two, three, four, five;
> two-one, two-two, two-three, two-four, two-five...

ACT ONE

Scene One

Nightfall and moonrise. A small HEDGEHOG snuffles in a patch of grass. Hears a sound and slips away.

SIX ADULT NEANDERTHALS shuffle in. The sixth Neanderthal is holding the hand of a CHILD. Perhaps we see them first coming in the distance. They have tattered feathers sewn into their clothing and walnut pendants around their necks. They are whistle-singing a call-in concert, the second group overlapping the first: fiu prrt fiu prrt fiu prrt fiu fiu fiu. It's a weird mourning song, sung for their fellows and themselves.

(This song is derived from the slow-down call of a Pied Butcherbird.)

NEANDER 1/3/5: Fiu/ fiu, fiuuu, fi-iufiufiu. (sick, sick, dying, death.)

NEANDER 2/4/6: /Prrt, prrt, prrt. (all day, all night, wait.)

NEANDER 1/3/5: Fiu/ fiu, fiuuu, fi-iufiufiu.

NEANDER 2/4/6: /Prrt. Prrt, prrt.

NEANDER 1: *(Dies.)*

NEANDER 2: *(Dies.)*

NEANDER 3: *(Dies.)*

NEANDER 4: *(Dies.)*

NEANDER 5: *(Dies.)*

NEANDER 6: *(Embraces the child and dies.)*

The NEANDERTHAL CHILD tugs at the MOTHER and tries to revive her, tries to lift up her mother's hand but it flops down. She gradually quickens the pace of the song until it becomes more anxious, pleading, insistent, plaintive, angry.

CHILD: Fiu prrt fiu prrrrrrt fiu prrrt fi-iufiufiu.

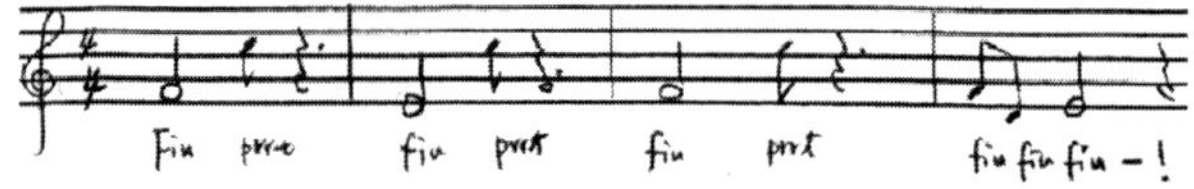

Fiu prrt fiu prrrrrrt fiu prrrt fi-iufiufiu.

Fiu prrt fiu prrrrrrt fiu prrrt fi-iufiufiu.

She goes quiet. The moon disappears, the night passes. Overcast. There are low rumbles of thunder and lightning in the distance. We hear CARRION BIRDS, their calls are low, guttural.

CARRION: Kwaaaawwik gwa!

CHILD: *(Pulling at her MOTHER.)* frrrrrrrrrr. frrrrrrrrrr.

CARRION: Kruk! Tawk! Kyewkyew!

The CHILD throws rocks at the birds to drive them away—

CHILD: Fiu prrt.

—but then the sound of someone approaching scares the birds off. The CHILD can't be seen.

An Early Modern Human couple enters. A woman, MO, and her mate, GORSE. They're not so young. GORSE is carrying both their spears. They each have a blade in a sheath on their shin. MO is carrying a small bundle.

GORSE: We walk far, Mo. All night we walk.

MO: We walk with moon, Gorse.

GORSE: Moon not here, Mo. Clouds here. Day here. Rain near.

MO: Moon there. *(Pointing up.)*

GORSE: Ne, Mo. All clouds.

MO: *(To her knees.)* Here.

GORSE: *(Sniffs.)* Some animal die here, Mo. Good people lie not here.

MO: Here, Gorse.

GORSE: *(Sniffs.)* Pah.

MO: Dig.

GORSE: Ne.

MO: *(Offers the bundle.)* Hold.

GORSE: Gah. *(Digs.)* Why not lie he near good people, Mo? Why here? Why way, way, way here?

MO: We walk with moon, Gor—

GORSE: Big animal come, smell me, smell you, eat me, eat you. You die. I die. Good People? Far! We die here. Die die die—

MO: Gorse— *(Shakes her head.)*

GORSE: —die.

MO: We walk here with moon. Moon see this child walk one straight night and see here, where he swim in earth. This child; blood.

GORSE: Yeh, this child...
Blood.

MO: I; you; child. Blood.
Here. Hold.

She gives him the bundle.

GORSE: Ah!

MO: This heart flows, here;
This eye flows, wet;
This child live, here: *(Her heart.)*
He: Cal.

GORSE: He: Cal.

MO: Walk, Cal;
Play, Cal;
Swim in earth—

GORSE: —Cal.

GORSE lays the bundle into the hole. Covers it with dirt.

MO: We blood, Gorse.

GORSE: We blood… Mo.

MO: *(Her hand is out, empty.)* Here: Eat salt.

GORSE touches her hand, kisses his fingers.

There is a flash of lightning. GORSE looks up, while MO's eye is drawn to some movement on the ground.

MO: Oh. What? (sees) Piper!

GORSE: What?

The NEANDERTHAL CHILD ducks away and hides.

MO: Piper! There!

GORSE: Piper?

MO: There!

GORSE: Yeh?

They investigate. There is a low rumble of thunder. MO gets close.

GORSE: *(Sniffs.)* Puh. Pipers die here. Guh.

MO: Why they here? long road here big water.

GORSE: What? Pipers not at big water.

MO: Pipers at big water, Gorse.

GORSE: Why?

MO: I not know. All pipers walk big water. They walk with Moon, Moon not say why.

GORSE: Moon not say why. Who know why.

MO: And this pipers die here. *(This is plural: they never say "these.")*

GORSE: And you see one here live?

MO: Child, yeh. Small.

GORSE: Where?

They look around. The NEANDERTHAL CHILD pops up and tries to run. Another flash of lightning.

CHILD: *(Trill not vocalized.)* prrrrrrrrrrrrrrrr.

MO: *(Struck.)* Child! Good!

GORSE: *(Scaring child.)* Gah! Gah!

MO: Nay, Gorse!

CHILD: *(Runs, cowers.)* prrrrrrrrr.

MO: Hold, Gorse, hold.

GORSE: I hold.

MO: *(Smacks him.)* She fear you.

GORSE: Yow ow.

MO: Where she?

GORSE: There, Mo.

MO: Where?

GORSE: There! *(Not with the bodies.)*

MO: Here, chicky-chick.

(Low rumble of thunder.)

MO: Here, chicky-chicky-chick.

GORSE: What if pipers near, Mo?

MO: Sh.
Here, Chick.

GORSE: Mo.

MO: Come, chicky-chicky-chick.

GORSE: That chick not come, Mo.

MO: Come, chicky-chicky-chick.

GORSE: Mo. No, Mo. This piper.
Big. Piper. Bite. Ow.

MO: Sit, Gorse.

GORSE: What?

MO: *(She sits.)* Sit.

GORSE: Gah.

MO is holding still with her hand extended. GORSE walks to the edge of the space, finally sits. It starts to rain. It rains more. Thunder, lightning. MO doesn't move.

GORSE: Mo.

MO: Come, Chicky.

The rain stops eventually. The sun comes out. They hear the CARRION BIRDS.

CARRION 1: *(Off.)* Kwaaaawwik!

CARRION 2: *(Off.)* Krk.

GORSE: Gah! birds.

He throws stones at them. The CHILD appears, throwing a stone. She crouches down by her mother.

GORSE: There, Mo: she stand, she fight. She good. We wet, we dirty, we walk back Good People, yeh?

MO: Sh, Guh.

GORSE: We not walk back.

CARRION: *(Off.)* Kwaaaak!

GORSE: *(Throws a stone.)* Rotten snake birds. I dig.

He takes a stick and goes to dig. Starts to take the bodies.

MO: Come, Chicky.

CHILD: Fiu prrt fiu prrrrrt.

MO: Come, Chicky chick. Come, Chicky chicky chick.

CHILD: Fiu prrrt fi-iufiufiu.

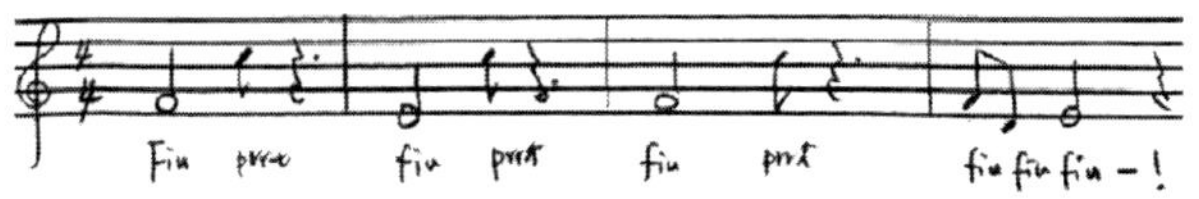

MO: Come here, chicky.

GORSE: Piper child hold mother, Mo. See?

MO: Mother who die, Gorse.

GORSE: Piper pull mother, Mo. Piper lie with mother. Wipe this. We walk back.

MO: That mother dust, ashes.
This—... mother… live.

GORSE: Nay, Mo.

MO: Come, chicky chick. What for sit with dust and ashes?

GORSE continues to take the bodies.

GORSE: Auch.

The CHILD is wearing a pendant—two acorn caps fixed together by the sticky goo inside them. She holds it out, gestures at her mother, too exhausted to explain in the way she will later.

CHILD: Fiu prrrt fi-iufiufiu.

MO: That? What is that?

CHILD: Prrt.

GORSE: Mo.

MO approaches the child. The child allows it. MO touches the acorn. Pulls the two pieces apart. The CHILD takes the salve and touches the mother's face. Then looks back at MO.

CHILD: Fiu prrt.

GORSE: Nay, child. Mother die.

MO: Mother, die, child.

MO closes the acorn.

CHILD: fi-iufiufiu.

MO: *(Steps back, gets low.)* Come, chicky chicky. *(She holds out a morsel.)* Come eat.

CHILD looks back and forth between MO's hand with food and her MOTHER.

CHILD: Fiu prrt fiu prrrrrrt.

MO: Eat, Chicky.

CHILD: Fiu prrrt fi-iufiufiu.

She lets go of her mother's hand, takes the morsel and eats. GORSE takes the body off. MO steps back again as GORSE returns. She offers her breast.

MO: Come, chick chicky chick. Come suck, chicky chick.

GORSE: Ne, Mo.

MO: Yeh, Gorse.

GORSE: Ne, Mo.

He takes his bladder of water, tosses it at the CHILD. The CHILD drinks.

CHILD: *(Drinks.)* Hmhmthmthmhmthmhmhmthmthmhm.

MO: Gorse.

GORSE: Big piper chick there, Mo. Big. Piper. Not child you belly, Mo.
Wipe this. Moon not give you this child.

MO: Cloud stick give this child.

GORSE: What?

MO: Burn stick, cloud stick. In sky. In rain. *(Lightning gesture.)* Pow.

GORSE: If cloud stick give this child, then Moon say no.

MO: Nay, Gorse. Moon say yes; Moon say yes.

GORSE: Nay, Mo.

MO: *(To CHILD.)* You. I. Suck at sun-sleep.

GORSE: No, Mo.

MO: Sun at foot. *(To CHILD.)* You. I. Moon. Stars. *(Gestures breastfeeding.)*

GORSE: You. She. Clouds. Rain.
Night come, animals come, eat me, eat you, eat pipers, eat chick.
We all die.
Die die die die die.

Scene Two

Sunset. Clear sky. MO is offering the child, now called CHICKY, small bits of food.

MO: No clouds, Gorse. No rain.

GORSE: No moon.

MO: Bah.

GORSE: *(Eating small, muttering.)* Hm. Good People kill we. They wipe we. They fight we they throw we they push we they wash. And we die.

MO: Chicky eat. Good.

CHICKY: *(Eats.)* Hmmhmthmhmnmnmthmhm.

MO: *(Eats small.)* Say: eat.

CHICKY: *(Eats. Pants. Drinks from Gorse's bladder.)* Hmhmthmthmhmthmhmhm.

MO: Say: Hmmm-ma.

CHICKY: Hmhmthmhmhmnmnm.

MO: Say: *(Indicating herself.)* Hm-maa. Ma. Maaa. Ma.

CHICKY: Hmthmn. *(Eats, very quiet hums, trills.)* Ete oto ete pee-yoo-tsay pee-yoo-tsay | Ete oto ete pee-yoo-tsay pee-yoo-tsay | Ete oto ete pee-yoo-tsay pee-yoo-tsay pee-yoo-tsay.

GORSE: Wha?

CHICKY: *(Whistles, hums, trills.)* Ete oto ete pee-yoo-tsay pee-yoo-tsay | Ete oto ete pee-yoo-tsay pee-yoo-tsay | Ete oto ete pee-yoo-tsay pee-yoo-tsay pee-yoo-tsay.

GORSE: Piper sing one-two-three.

MO: Good green grass.

GORSE: Piper sing one-two-three, Mo.
(Takes up drum, plays in 3/4 time.)
See?

MO: Gorse.

GORSE: I play. You sing with.

MO: Pah.

GORSE: Come, you.

MO: Fah,

GORSE: Wait.

CHICKY: *(Whistles, hums, trills.)* Ete oto ete pee-yoo-tsay pee-yoo-tsay—

GORSE: *(Sings under his breath, plays, 6/4 time, on drum.)*
Ducky-ducky-ducky duck duck duck, duck duck duck.
Ducky-ducky-ducky duck duck duck, duck duck duck, duck duck duck.

CHICKY: *(Starts over.)* Ete oto ete pee-yoo-tsay pee-yoo—

GORSE: Ducky-ducky-ducky duck duck duck, duck duck duck.
Ducky-ducky-ducky duck duck duck, duck duck duck, duck duck duck.

MO: *(3/4 time, joining Gorse and the child.)*
Cooo coo-coo, cooo coo-coo, cooo coo-coo.

CHICKY has stopped, watches.

GORSE: *(Continuing same rhythm.)*
Mama-mama-mama ma ma ma, ma ma ma.
Mama-mama-mama ma ma ma, ma ma ma.
Mama-mama-mama ma ma ma, ma ma ma, ma ma ma.

MO: *(Joining GORSE.)*
Fah fa-fa, fah fa-fa, fah fa-fa, fah fa-fa.

CHICKY eats.

MO/GORSE: *(Slowly realizing they've taken over the CHILD's song.)*
Mama-mama-mama, fah fa-fa, fah fa-fa.
Mama-mama-mama, fah fa-fa, fah fa-fa.
Mama-mama-mama... fah fa... fa.
Mama... mama...
Fa.

CHILD pants. MO gives bladder to child.

CHICKY: *(Drinks.)* Hmhmthmthmmhmhmhmhm.

MO eats small. GORSE eats small.

CHICKY: *(More quietly.)* Ete oto ete pee-yoo-tsay pee-yoo-tsay | Ete oto ete pee-yoo-tsay pee-yoo-tsay | Ete oto ete pee-yoo-tsay pee-yoo-tsay pee-yoo-tsay.

Blackout.

Scene Three

Daytime. Early Modern Human community: the "Good People."

BABY: *(Off.)* Mmwa! mwaa! mwaa! mwaa! mwaa! mwaa!

GRAN: Neh, neh, here. *(Instructions to a YOUNG WOMAN with a BABY.)*
Wash skin. Not sew.

YOUNG WOMAN: Neh?

GRAN: Ne! Dirty! Smell bad. See? Smell!

YOUNG WOMAN: Yeh.

GRAN: Fat here. See? Ick. Bad. Wash this good. *(Sits.)*

YOUNG WOMAN: You smell bad, old woman.

GRAN: Eh?

YOUNG WOMAN: Yeh. I wash good.

GRAN: Hold one day, one night: when dry, sew.

YOUNG WOMAN: Yeh.

BABY: Mmwa! mwaa! mwaa!

TWO MEN with a big carcass enter.

MAN 1: Pull.

MAN 2: I pull.

MAN 1: Pull!

MAN 2: Faw.

DOG: *(Off.)* Hurrrrrr, grrrrrrp. Yip!

MAN 1: *(Giving up the task.)* Ne, hold. Here come Gorse.

DOG: *(Off.)* Yip! Yip!

MAN 2: Oh yeh. And Mo. They walk long walk.

MAN 1: Pah.

MAN 2: Hold. I count three.

MAN 1: Three?

MAN 2: One with Mo... Child.

MAN 1: Neh, not child. They child die.

MAN 2: Yeh, yeh, I know. They child die.

MAN 1: Good green guts. That piper. Mo hold hand piper.

MAN 2: Nay.

MAN 1: I spit.

MAN 2: I see. Piper child. Mo pull piper. Piper pull back, pull heavy.

MAN 1: That not good. Gorse think that good? That not good.

MAN 2: And why that not good say if Gorse and Mo think that good?

MAN 1: Moon think that not good.

MAN 2: How you know?

MAN 1: Moon say. Moon say that not good.

MAN 2: Why?

MAN 1: Moon not say why. Who know why. We live. They die.

MAN 2: Pipers die?

MAN 1: They swell belly, walk big water, die. You not know that?

MAN 2: Yeh, yeh, I know.

MAN 1: Pipers die. We live.
We wipe this.
(Calling to all.)
SEE! PIPER!

MAN 2: Uh ANIMAL!

GRAN: *(Startled.)* What what?

MAN 2: PIPER!

GRAN: *(Sees.)* Good green guts. What this for, Gorse?

MAN 2: PIPER HERE! ANIMAL!

MAN 1: ALL GOOD PEOPLE COME PUSH THIS PIPER BACK!

GRAN: Small piper, huh.

MAN 2: PUSH PIPER AND ROTTEN BAD PEOPLE BACK!

GRAN: Rotten bad people Gorse and Mo, yeh?

She stands.

And I one old bad smell here, yeh?

OTHERS: *(Various.)* THROW! FIGHT! FALL! SPIT! DIRTY! STAB!

GRAN: *(Gathers things.)* I, I, I, I, yeh. One bad smell and rotten bad people.

OTHERS: PUSH! *(They coalesce into a rhythm.)*

THROW FIGHT SPIT STAB PUSH!
WASH!

THROW FIGHT SPIT STAB PUSH!
WASH!

THROW FIGHT SPIT STAB PUSH!
WASH!

GRAN exits.

OTHERS: THROW FIGHT SPIT STAB PUSH!
WASH!

Scene Four

GORSE enters.

GORSE: Skid! Piss! Fug!
Spit. Spit, Mo. Gah!
Fug.
We not with Good People.
We not Good People.
When people not Good People, people die.
We die.

MO enters, yanking at CHICKY.

MO: Come. Come.

CHICKY: *(Low trill.)* Krrrrrrrrrrrrrrr

MO: Hm-maa. Come.
Come, chick. Come come. Come!

GORSE: Mo!

MO: Here, chick. *(Tries to lift her.)*

CHICKY: KrrrrrMwhAAAA—!

MO: Neh, here—

CHICKY: —AAAA! *(Smack, smack, smack.)*

MO: Ah! Ugh!

CHICKY: *(Runs.)*
aheehaHAHAHAHEEHEEHAMWAHAHA!

CHICKY exits.

MO: Snake child. Ug! Fug.

GORSE: Mo.

MO: Heart.

GORSE: Gah.

MO: Heave.

GORSE: Mo.

MO: Rain.

GORSE: That child walk with you? Ne.
That child walk with I? Ne.
That child walk with Good People? Neh!
You not ma that one, Mo. You not that one ma.
I not that one fa.
We hold child, Mo: he die.

MO: Moon give new child.

GORSE: Neh. Moon not give you this child.

MO: Cloud stick that burn give new ch—

GORSE: Yeh. Not Moon. Cloud stick give you this child. Cloud stick burn I, you, piper. And Moon: Moon know. Good people know. We child die. We see child die.

MO: He Cal.

GORSE: He: Cal.

MO: Rain.

GORSE: Cal swim in earth.
See?

Looks off in the direction CHICKY went.

That child not—*(Looks closer.)* Good green grass.
(Shouts off.) Blood River flow! Flow, chick! You hear?
Ne— Blood River pull you in, chick. You not swim, you not float.
Blood River kill you! You hear? YOU HEAR?

...
Spit, Mo. I fear water.
I fear water, Mo!
Gah!

He runs off.

MO: Cloud stick not give you this new child, Gorse. Blood River give you this child. *(Looks closer.)*
Good green grass, Gorsey.

Pause.

CHICKY: *(Off.)* heehehehahahahaaahaa!

GORSE enters, wet, with the wet child.

CHICKY: Ffrrrrrrrg! *(Scratches.)* Heehahaheeeha! Frgg!

GORSE: Child. Ow.

CHICKY: *(Hits, bites.)* FrgrrfrgrrfrgrrrRRRRGhahahaha haha-hehehehahahaharrfrg-

GORSE: Spit skid. Yow!

CHICKY: *(Bites.)* Grrrrrphhffffffffngr—

GORSE: Good green guts fug.

CHICKY: —rrrhahahahahahHAHAHAHAHEEHEE-HA.

CHICKY and GORSE stop, poised in opposition.

MO: Good father you, Gorse.

GORSE: *(To CHICKY.)* River water not walk with you, hear? River water pull you in. River kill you.

CHICKY: *(Raspberry.)*

GORSE: Oh fuh. *(Wipes face.)*

CHICKY: HahahehahahahehahaHEḤA!

GORSE: All wet, Mo—this little piper.

CHICKY: HahohahehahahahaaaaaeeeeeeHAAA!
(Shivers, cold.)
tsetsetsetse.

GORSE: Mo, where we hold small bark? You hold small bark in that skin, yeh?

CHICKY: *(Trill vocalized.)* rrrrrrrrrrrrrr.

MO: Here? *(Her bag.)*
I hold bark. I hold small bark.
(Pulls out a garment. She's not sure.)
Cal bark.

GORSE: *(He's sure.)* Cal bark, yeh. I know.

MO: Cal.

GORSE: I know that. Give bark this child, yes? This child wet.

MO: ... Yes. Yes. Give... this child.

CHICKY: rrrrrrr.

GORSE: Here. Hold.

CHICKY: tsetsetsetsetse.

GORSE: Mo?

MO: Yeh.

She gives him the garment.

GORSE: Child? Chicky: you cold.

CHICKY: tstststs. tstststs.

MO: Chicky.

GORSE: Hold.

He tries to undress/dress her.

CHICKY: Rrrraarrrrgha.

GORSE: Piss. Fug.

MO: Gorse.

CHICKY: Rrgha. Rrgha. ARGHARGHAH!

GORSE: Ugh. Oh. *(Stops, gives up, rationalizes.)* Ah, ne, she not cold, yeh? This one live wet, yeh?

MO: She cold, Gorse!

GORSE: Pipers not cold, Mo! Thick skin not freeze. Hair. I see—

MO: All animals cold when wet, Gorse.

GORSE: N—

MO: When child!

GORSE: Mo, you say that bark Cal bark—

MO: All animals. This child wet. Hair wet. Skin wet. Bark wet.

GORSE: This child live wet, laugh wet, kill we wet.

MO: Gorse; You: legs. I: head.

GORSE: Yeh. Yeh. I hold.

They try to undress her. They don't succeed.

CHICKY: FrrroooomoooooowaaaaaaAAAAAAAH-HHHHH!

GORSE: Urgh.

MO: Urrgh!

CHICKY: Grr, grr, grrrrrr, frrroooomoooooowaaaaaaAAAh—

GORSE: Good green guts, Mo.

CHICKY: *(Runs, trills.)* HeeheeheehahahahaHAHAHEEHEEHEHA-RRRRRRRRR! Hoo. Frrroo. rrrrrrrrrrrrrrrr rrrrrrrrrrrrRRrrrrrRrrr.
(Stops.)

Fiu prrt fiu prrt. Fiu prrt fi-iufiufiu.

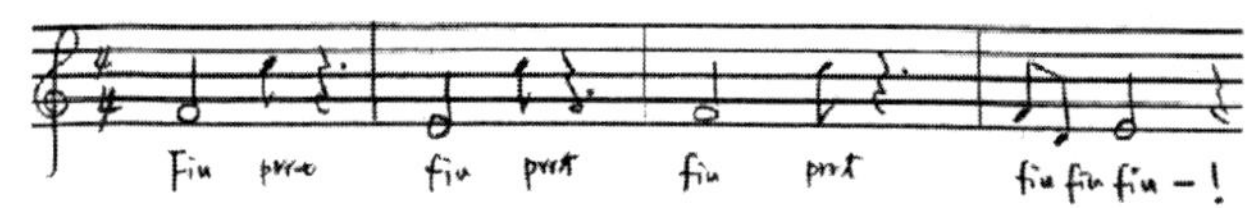

MO: Wha?

GORSE: Wha?
. . .
Ma?

GRAN enters, laden.

GRAN: I, you, you I, Gorse, Mo.

GORSE: Ma—

GRAN: Gorse, I—

GORSE: What for, Ma?

GRAN: Come with you.

GORSE: No. No, no, no. Walk back, Ma. You die here, Ma. Walk back.

GRAN: Come with you, Gorse. You father. Mo mother. I: Gran. I Gran.

GORSE: Ma.

GRAN: ... Gorse.

GORSE: Ma.

GRAN: Why?

GORSE: Moon not say why, Ma. Walk back.

GRAN: *(Drops everything.)* I you, you, I, Gorse; Mo.

GRAN turns. Trips, recovers. Exits.

CHICKY: *(Runs.)* Frrrrrrrrrrrr. frrrrrrrrrrr. Frrrrrrrrrr!

CHICKY exits after GRAN.

MO: Gorse.

CHICKY reappears, holding GRAN by the hand.

CHICKY: Fiu prrt fiu prrt. Fiu prrt fi-iufiufiu.

MO: Gran.

GORSE: Gran.

GRAN: Child.

MO: Chicky.

GRAN: Chicky child.
Chicky child.
I squeeze you. I squeeze you!

CHICKY: *(Picks up garment.)* Fiu prrt fiu prrt. Fiu prrt fi-iufiufiu.

GRAN: You say I bark you? I?

CHICKY: Fiu prrt.

GRAN: I give you this bark, yeh, child. I not fear you.

CHICKY: Fiu prrt.

(If GRAN needs more time to dress CHICKY, she could sing a Good People children's song: "Wind blow/Wind blow/Clouds come count clouds/One, two, three, four, five.")

MO: *(Watching.)* Heart.
Heavy.
Heart.

GORSE: Fear not Ma, Mo.

MO: Ne.

GORSE: Fight not Ma, Mo.

MO: Spit.

GORSE: Mo.

MO: Stick.

Scene Five

CARRION BIRDS come and go.

CARRION: Krk. Krrrk. Kwak.

CHICKY is running in her new clothes.

CHICKY: HoohahahahaheehahaHEEHA

MO enters.

MO: Chicky chick chick.

GORSE enters.

Chicky chicky chick chick chick chick —

GORSE: Mo.

MO: Chick chicky chick —.

GORSE: Good green guts, Mo, we walk here!
Child come hold you when...

MO: When?
When?

GORSE: …when child come hold you.

GRAN enters.

CHICKY: *(To GRAN.)* Dee-dee dee-dee tee-uwhit. *(This is derived from a blackbird call.)*

dee-dee dee-dee tee-u-whit !

GRAN: I squeeze you.

CHICKY: Tee-uwhit.

MO: Gah.

GRAN: Ne, I not hold you, Chicky. I walk. You walk.

CHICKY: Tee-uwhit.

GRAN: We walk.

CHICKY: Fiu prrt fiu prrt. Fiu prrrrt fi-iufiufiu.

GRAN: I squeeze you. Squeeeeze.

MO: I scratch. Ugh. Hair.

GORSE: *(Drops gear.)* We sit. We eat. We sleep.
I hunt sticks.

He goes to collect sticks. MO squats and starts delousing her hair and flicking lice away, despondently.

MO: *(Finding one.)* Louse. *(Another louse.)* Louse. *(Another.)* Louse.
Louse. Louse.

CHICKY: *(To MO.)* Fiu prrt fiu prrt.

MO: What?

CHICKY: Fiu prrrrt fi-iufiufiu.

MO: Louse? *(Gives it.)*

CHICKY: *(Eats.)* Mmnmnmnmthmthmthm.

MO: *(Delighted.)* Ha! *(Appalled.)* Oh. Here. *(Another.)*

CHICKY: *(Eats.)* Mmnmnmthm.

MO: Come, chicky. Eat.

CHICKY: *(Grooms Mo, eats.)* Fiu prrt fiu prrt. Mmnmnmnmthmthmthm.

MO: Ha! Say "eat."

CHICKY: Fiu prrt fiu prrt.

MO: "Eat."

CHICKY: Mmnmnmnm.

GRAN finds a louse in her own hair, offers to CHICKY. MO smacks her hand. GRAN offers again.

MO: *(Smacks hand away.)* Gran!

GRAN: Pah.

MO: Gran. I give meat, I mother.

GRAN: Meat? Louse not meat, Mo.

MO: Gran—

GORSE: *(Trying to balance three standing sticks.)* Rub not salt in, Gran.

GRAN: Bah.

CHICKY: *(Grooms MO, eats.)* Fiu prrt fiu prrt. Mmnmnmnm.

GORSE: *(Balancing three sticks.)* Stick one... stick two... stick three... There.

He goes to find more. A TOAD calls from a patch of grass.

TOAD: Croac... croac...

CHICKY: *(Eating another louse.)* Mmnmnmnmthmthmthm.

TOAD: Rrriiiiivvet... rrriiiiivvet...

GRAN: I hear small fat animal, Mo.

MO: Yeh, Gran.

GRAN: Meat. Chicky hands in you hair, Mo. I—...

MO: Good green guts, GRAN: kill that small fat animal.

GRAN: Yeh.

TOAD: Rrriiiiivvet.

GRAN: *(To the TOAD.)* I heear yoou..

TOAD: Croac—

GRAN: *(Attacks.)* Die! small fat animal... *(Misses.)* No. No. Where?

MO: There!

GRAN: I kill you! *(Tries.)* No!

MO: There!

CHICKY is trying to reach for the lice, but MO has joined GRAN in the hunt. The TOAD continues to elude them.

GRAN: There!

MO: There!

They exit. CHICKY is left.

CHICKY: Rriiivvet.
Rriivvet.

GORSE enters with more sticks to balance. CHICKY watches him.

GORSE: Fire near. Stick four... stick five... stick two-one... No. This stick one-one, stick two-one at... *(Gestures "later," then shakes head, confused):*
Heavy head.
(Resumes.)
Stick one-one... stick one-two... stick one-three... stick one-fo—

CHICKY: *(Runs through the sticks.)*
Heeheeheeheeheeheehahahaheehaha
HAHAHEEHEEHOO!

GORSE: Gah!

CHICKY: *(Runs circles.)* HAHEEHEEHAHEHAHA-HAHAHAHAHAHEEHA

GORSE: Mo!

CHICKY: *(Hops.)* Ha hee ha hee ha hee ha!

GORSE: Piper! Pah! Piper! Mo!

MO enters with GRAN, toadless.

MO: Huh?

GORSE: Small one kill fire! And laugh!
I count sticks, small one run, kill sticks, laugh.

MO: Kill sticks?

GORSE: Kill sticks kill fire! See?

MO: That stick not die, Gorse. We die, if we not eat.

GORSE: Gah! I hunt.

He takes up spear, exits.

CHICKY: Heehaheehee

She exits, following.

MO: Nay, Chick.

GRAN: Nayo, Mo.

MO: Gorse hunt, Gran. Chicky—

GRAN: Chicky walk with father when he hunt. Good, ne?

MO: Ne. Chicky hunt father. Not good. Sun near foot. Not good.

GRAN: Good green guts.

Scene Six

There is undergrowth.

HIDDEN HEDGEHOG: *(Barely audible.)* tt, t, t, t, t, t,t .

GORSE enters.

GORSE: *(Whispers.)* Small animal.
Sun near foot. Night come.

HIDDEN HEDGEHOG: t, tt, t, t, t,t, t, t.

GORSE: Here... there... ah... there.

HIDDEN HEDGEHOG rustles.

CHICKY: *(Enters, barely audible.)* t, tt, t, t, t.

GORSE: *(Turns, finger to lips.)* Shhhh.

CHICKY: t, tt.

HIDDEN HEDGEHOG rustles.

GORSE: *(Spears into undergrowth.)* Ha! Die die die. Eat. We eat!

CHICKY claps.

GORSE: Ye. We eat.

CHICKY: Fiu prrt fiu prrt. *(Celebrates.)*

GORSE: *(Pushes spear, holds it.)* You eat. Eat. Say "eat."

CHICKY: Fiu prrt.

GORSE: Pah. We eat.

CHICKY: *(Grins big teeth.)*

GORSE: *(Grins big teeth.)*

CARRION BIRDS come to periphery.

CARRION 1: Krrrk.

CARRION 2: Kwak.

CARRION BIRDS withdraw.

CHICKY: Krk. Krk.
Krk.
(To GORSE, explaining. This is derived from the song of a hermit thrush.) Ta tsa-ha-dum twee du-hum | taa twee duhm | um twee-dum | tsa-hee-ha-doo | tsa ha tse dee | -tsee ha-doo.

GORSE: *(Hesitating over corpse.)* What?

CHICKY: *(Pointing off.)* Krk. Krk.

GORSE: Birds?

CHICKY: Ta tsa-ha-dum twee du-hum.

GORSE: Birds go. We not fight them. Dirty birds. Animal die, swell, bad smell, they eat. Neh. They go.

CHICKY: — taa twee duhm.

CARRION: *(Unseen wing flutter.)* Erk!

GORSE: You and I walk back. *(Reaches down for quarry.)*

CHICKY: Èh! Èh! AAERRRRRGGGHHHH!

GORSE: Hold! Ow! What? *(She's lunging for the carcass in his hand.)*

CHICKY: Èh! Èh!

GORSE: You eat here? That what? Belly bite? Yeh? Eat?

CHICKY: Èh. Èh.

GORSE: Hold, Chicky.

CHICKY: Ta tsa-ha-dum twee du-hum—

GORSE: Hold.
(Digs into carcass.)
Here, you.
(Offers.)
Eat. Say—

CHICKY: Èh! Èh! *(Takes it.)* AAERGH! *(Hurls it away.)*

GORSE: Wha—? Throw MEAT?
UGH! YOU!
Walk back Mo, you. Walk back Gran, you. Walk back!
Throw meat, ugh, bad. You throw meat, I throw you, you!
Say "eat," you. You say "ea—"

CHICKY attacks, smacks, pinches, bloody hands.

GORSE: Ow ow ow!
I hold meat this hand, I hold you this hand, we walk back, you not—

CHICKY: AaaaiiieeeeeeeaaaiiieeeeeeEEEEEEEEE!

GORSE: Mo!
You say "eat"!
Mo! Mo!

Exeunt.

Scene Seven

MO and GRAN.

GRAN: Here they come.

GORSE and CHICKY enter.

GORSE: Mo!

GRAN: Blood at you nose there, Gorse.

GORSE: Mo! This child snake. This small child not play, no!
Snake!
Kill fire.
Fight fa!
Throw meat. Meat!
This child not straight, Mo. Animal. Piper.
Hold this little piper.
(To the child.) You, little one; you kill not us this night.
(To MO and GRAN.) Yeh?

MO: Yeh, yeh.

GRAN: Yeah.

GORSE: Here. Hold.
(Takes up three sticks, balances them.)
Stick one, stick two... stick three.
(Adds more.) ... Stick four... Stick five... Stick two-one— er, no, stick one-one, stick—

CHICKY gets away from MO and GRAN, .

GRAN/MO: Chicky! No!

CHICKY: *(Scatters sticks, as before, imitating birds.)*
Krick! Krac!

GORSE: Neh! Neh!

CHICKY: KahahahahaHAHAHAHA, KRICK! KRAWWK!
(Imitates carrion bird.)
KrAHAHAHAHAHEEHEEHEEIIIEEE-AAIIIAAAAAAHAHA!

GORSE: *(To sky, fists beat ground.)* Gah gah gah gaaaaaaah!

CHICKY: *(Flaps, runs in circles.)* KrK! Krk! Krkkrkrkkrrrawk.

MO: "Krick krawk?"

GRAN: "Krick krawk," yeh.

MO: "Krick krawk."

GRAN: Warm night. Stars there. We good.

CHICKY: Krawk krawk!

GORSE: Ah, moon. Gah.

MO: We good, Gran.

GRAN: Here, Gorse: eat salt.

GORSE: Ugh.

CHICKY slows circles, slows circles, stops, drops, sleeps.

MO: Chicky sleep. Good.

GRAN and MO settle in. GORSE calms. Approaches MO for sex.

GORSE: *(Quiet.)* I lie with you, woman.

MO: Ne, Gorse.

GORSE: Yeh, Mo.

MO: Neh!

GORSE drops. Sleeps.

MO: *(Sits up.)* Gorse. Husband.

GORSE snores.

MO: *(Stands, comes to front.)* It's cold.

Moon. Are you looking at me? Can you see me? Moon. You are looking at me. You can see me. I have these thoughts, I don't know how to express them. Do you understand anyway? Even if I have not found all the words for things that are buried deep within here? *(She knocks on her head.)*

I must tell you that we are in great peril. The great peril of love. She will not bind herself to us. I am failing as a mother. With Gorse she fights and I cannot calm her. She would love me if I were better but I am not good and so she does not love me. Naturally, I was not meant to be a mother because you see my child died. You see. My child died. And in a lightning strike of love I claimed another child. And now this one does not bind herself to me because I am not fit to be a mother. And so we are going to lose everything. Everything. We are going to die.

But if we die, she dies. And she would have died if we had not taken her. So what choice did we have? Watch her die or else walk with her towards death.

Though it is true we are not walking with her. She is running away from us and we are running after her. Running very very fast towards death.

Should we have left her? Moon? Should we have just left her to die?

No! No I will not I would never I will never!

If only she could speak.

She does not have language. She just... hums and whistles like birds do. It's pretty but, what is it? Who is she? What is she? Is she a bird?

There is one hope that is also a hurt. She does love Gorse's mother. I am grateful for this and it also hurts. Oh, it hurts. She loves her easily. Why will she not love me? What does Gran have that I do not have? Other than clearly she was fit to be a mother because she has a son he is Gorse. But what else could there be something else? Could it be because she is weak and so they can both be weak together?

Moon, I cannot be weak. Moon, I have to be strong. But when I hold her and she struggles, I want to put her down and I want to lie down and go to sleep and let the big beasts come.

It's cold tonight, Moon. Big beasts are hungry and we have no fire. Bah. Pah.

Scene Eight

Day. A bit of time has passed. GORSE enters, his spear raised. There is undergrowth.

CARRION 1: *(In and out, a flutter.)* Krawk.

CHICKY enters, a rope tied around her waist, pulled taut, off.

HIDDEN RABBIT: Piu, piu, piu, piu, piu.

CHICKY: Piu piu piu.

GORSE: *(Whisper.)* Gah!

MO enters, holding other end of the rope. GRAN enters. Perhaps she is holding too.

MO: Gorse.

GORSE: *(Whisper.)* I hunt. Hold she.

MO: I hold, fuh. Two days I hold. Two. She not laugh. I not laugh.

GORSE: I not laugh.

MO: Heart heavy.

GORSE: Not long.

MO: Fuh.

GORSE: Mrrg. Small animal not here, good green guts.

CHICKY: *(Barely audible.)* Piu, piu.

GORSE: You—

HIDDEN RABBIT: *(Barely audible.)* Piu, piu, piu.

GORSE: Oh.

A small CHICKY/RABBIT dialogue. GORSE kills it swiftly.

GORSE: *(To CHICKY.)* See? *(Picks up kill, waves it in front of the child.)*
Kill. I. This.
I kill this.
Smoke. I. This.
I smoke this.
Eat. I. This. I eat this.

MO: Gorse.

GORSE: Eat. One. Eat. Other. All eat!

He starts to move away with the dead rabbit.

CHICKY: iiiiiieeeeeeeeeeaaaaaaaah

(Runs, falls, slaps herself many times in head, face.)
eeeeeeeeeeeeeeeeeeeeaaaaaaaaaaa-
AAAAAAAAAAAAHAAAAA!-

MO: Chicky! Ne! Ne! No! No, Chicky.

GORSE: Stick one. Stick two.

CHICKY: AAAAAAAAAAAAAAH!

GORSE: Stick three.

MO: Gorse.

GORSE: Stick four, stick five. Er.

MO: Gorse!

GORSE: Mo?

MO: Give.
Give!

GORSE: What, give that piper this small dead animal? Neh.

MO: Yeh, Gorse.

GORSE: Neh, Mo: kill, I, this; skin, I—

MO: Here. *(Takes the rabbit.)*
Here. *(Gives it to CHICKY.)*
Here. *(Unties rope.)*
There.

GORSE: I die here. I die.

CHICKY: *(Explaining, as before.)* Ta tsa-ha-dum twee du-hum | taa twee duhm | -
(Puts rabbit back at its kill place.) um twee-dum | tsa-hee-ha-doo | tsa ha tse dee | -tsee ha-doo.

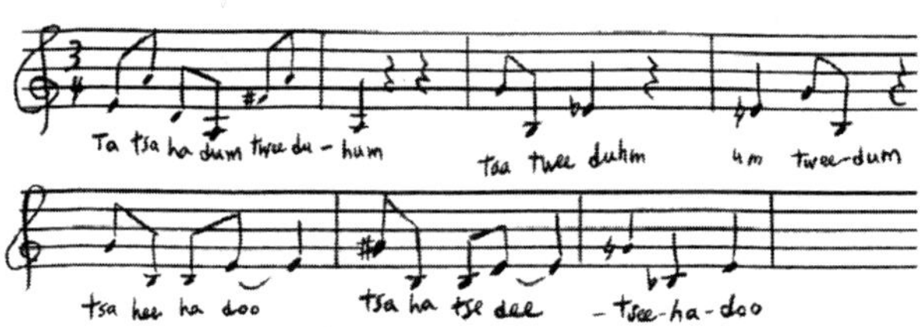

CHICKY exits.

GRAN: Ha ha ha, what? Ha ha, Chicky not eat that. Chicky say: "I not eat this small animal!" Ha ha ha.

GORSE: Clouds fly; wind blows: That piper splits this head.

MO: Gorse.

CHICKY re-enters, pushes GRAN off.

CHICKY: Fiu prrt fiu prrt fiuuu prrt fi-iufiufiu.

MO: Push not Gran, Chicky. Gran old woman.

GRAN: I walk. I walk back.

CHICKY returns, pushes MO.

MO: Yeh, Chicky, I walk with Gran, yeh, see?

They exit. CHICKY returns for GORSE.

GORSE: What for? Neh: say what for.

CHICKY: Ta tsa-ha-dum twee du-hum—

GORSE: Yeh.

He goes. There is a flutter of wings. A CARRION BIRD enters.

CARRION: Kwaaaawwik gwa!
Krk. Krrrk! Kwaaaawik!
Kruk! Tawk!

CHICKY enters running, aiming GORSE's spear precariously.

GORSE: *(Off.)* What? Ne!

MO: Hold, Gorse.

CHICKY: Eeeeeeeiiiiiiiiiaaaaaayyyyyiiiieeeeeh!

CARRION: *(Facing CHICKY.)* Kwaaawik!

CHICKY is trying to stab the bird with GORSE's spear. GORSE runs on, followed by MO and GRAN.

GORSE: Eeeeeiyow! *(Grabs his spear and stabs the carrion bird.)*

CARRION: Krrk! Kwaaaa.

GORSE: That big dirty bird, kill you, hear? Bite you, scratch you, kill you, eat you, hear? Pah!

CHICKY: Ta tsa-ha-dum twee du-hum | taa twee duhm- |
(Gives rabbit to GORSE.)
-um twee-dum | tsa-hee-ha-doo |
(Pulls at the feathers of the dead bird.)
tsa ha tse dee | -tsee ha-doo.
(Turns back to GORSE, holding a clutch of feathers still stuck to the wing.)
Krick! Krac!

GORSE: What? *(Plucks a feather.)* This?

CHICKY: *(Lays wing over one arm, poses, awkwardly.)* Fiu prrt fiu prrt fiuuu prrt fi-iufiufiu.

GORSE: *(To MO.)* Ah!

MO: Feathers!

GORSE: Chicky hunt feathers!

MO: Sew in bark, yeh? You sew feathers in bark.

GRAN: Hahahaha! *(Clap clap clap.)* Wings! Oh, I squeeze you.

GORSE: Wings.

GRAN: Wings!

MO: *(Teaching the word.)* Ffffeathers.

CHICKY: Ffffiu prrt fiu prrt fiuuu prrt fi-iufiufiu.

MO: Feathers.

CHICKY: *(Almost saying it.)* Fiuuu - rrrrrrrr.

MO: She say, she say!

GORSE: She not say.

MO: She say!

CHICKY: fi-iufiufiu.

Scene Nine

Straight through from previous scene. Down floats about. Working together, they have made a feathered garment for CHICKY. They put it on her. She is excited. Stands straight. Balls fists. Cries out.

CHICKY: Brrrrraaa!
(Stands straighter. Trills loud and slow and low.)
trrrrrrp, trrrrr-trrr trrrrrp.
trrrrrrp, trrrrr-trrr trr-trrp.

CHICKY stops, cocks ear, listens.

GRAN: Sing, child.

CHICKY listens.

GRAN: Sing, chicky-child; sing!

CHICKY closes her eyes, still listening. We might hear, very distantly, the response she is listening for.

CHICKY: trrrrrrp, trrrrr-trrr trrrrrp.
trrrrrrp, trrrrr-trrr trr-trrp.

MAMMOTH: *(Distant, unseen, low rumble.)*
Bgrrrbrgbgrrbbbbrrrrrrrbrrrr, brrgrbbr-bgrrr bgrbgrrr.
Bgrrrbrgbgrrbbbbrrrrrrrbrrrr, brrgrbbr-bgrrr bgrbgrrr-bgrr

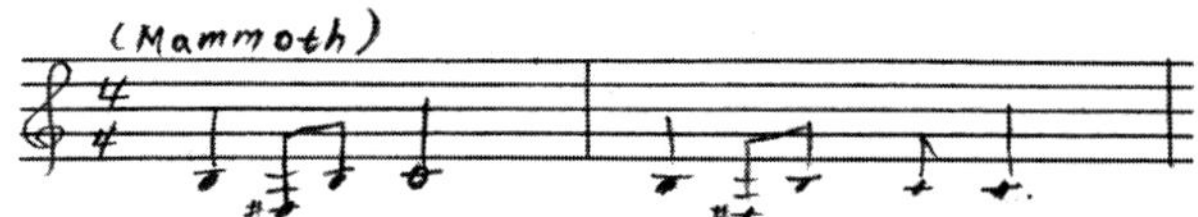

CHICKY: *(Laughs, then:)* trrrrrrp *(Then small trumpet.)*

MAMMOTH: Bgrrrbrgbgrrbbbbrrrrrrrbrrrr *(Then full trumpet before moving away.)*

CHICKY: *(Sits, plucks grass.)* Fiu prrrt.

MO: Big animal.

GORSE: Big.

MO: She not eat that.

GRAN: She not eat that big animal, no.

GORSE: Ne, she not eat that.

MO: Ne. she sing with that, she hear, laugh, play with that.

GORSE: Yeh.

MO: *(Approaching her proudly.)* Chicky-chick-chick.

CHICKY: *(Turns away.)* prrrt.

MO: I...
Ne. She not give heart this good day, Gorse. Not at I.

GORSE: She give heart at you, Mo. She give heart at you.

MO: She live with I. She not give heart at I. Why? Moon not say why. Who know why.

GORSE: Ne, Mo, she give heart at y—

MO: Gorse. I know. I say she not!
Dust. Ashes.

GORSE is despondent. Night is falling.

MO: Gorse.

GORSE: Nay, you say what you say.

MO: Ba!

GORSE looks up.

MO: *(Indicating.)* Sun at foot. Sun sleep.

GORSE: Oh.

MO: *(Mouthing it, pointing to CHICKY.)* Fire.

GORSE: Fire, yeh. Nay, Mo. I not fear Chicky. Wings, feathers, good. Chicky good. Chicky... fly. Good.

MO: Good. Chicky not kill us this day. You good.

GORSE: I good, Mo.

MO: Good.

GORSE: Sticks.

CHICKY: Fiu prrt fiu prrt.

GORSE: Stick one... Stick two... Stick three... ...
Stick four... ... Stick five...
Stick two-one. Ne.
(Laughs.)
I say "stick two-one" when I — when I say "stick five"
(Shakes head.) "Stick five, stick two-one." Nay, Gorse "Stick five, stick one-one." Yeh? Puh.

CHICKY: Heha.

GORSE: What for we say that? What for we say one-one when that, not two-one when that?
Stick one, stick one-one *(Shakes head.)* What for? Split this head.
(Resumes.)
Stick one-one... Stick one-two... sti—

CHICKY: *(Runs through the sticks.)* Heeheeheeheeheeheehahahaheehaha HAHAHEEHEEHOO!

GORSE: ...

CHICKY: *(Runs circles.)* HAHEEHEEHAHEHAHAHAHAHAHAHAHEEHA!

GORSE: ...

CHICKY: *(Hops.)* Ha hee ha hee ha hee ha!

MO: Chicky chicky.

CHICKY: *(Hops.)* Ha hee ha!

MO: Chicky Chick.

CHICKY: *(Hops.)* Ha hee ha.

MO: Oh, Chicky. Ah-ah-oh-ahh.

CHICKY: Ha hee. Fiu prrt fiu prrt fiuuu prrt fi-iufiufiu.

MO continues to try to get CHICKY to come. CHICKY continues to not come. Night falls.

Scene Ten

Darkness.

BEAR: Heuh! Heuhhhhuhh! Heuhhhhh! Heuuhhh! HEUUHHHHH!

CHICKY: *(Throaty.)* thweeeeeeet!

MO: Ahhgh!

GORSE: Mo! Where you!

CHICKY: thweeeeeeet!

GORSE: Chicky, back! Mo!

MO: Ahgh!

GORSE: Mo!

MO: Ahagh! Ahaghhhhhh! *(Back and forth with bear.)*

GORSE: Ahargh! Ergh!

MO: Oh! Oh. Ah.

BEAR: *(Injured, receding.)* Errrgh! Errrgh! Errrgggh!

GORSE: Chicky?

CHICKY: fiu prrrt.

GORSE: *(High keening.)* Hi hi hi hi hi hi hi hi hi hi hi hi. Mo. Hi hi hi hi hi Mo. hi hi hi hi hi hi.

Dim light. MO is lying face down, her knife drawn and bloody. GORSE is by her. Bloody spear on ground beside him. CHICKY is near, crouching and looking, fingering the pendant around her neck. She is feathered now. GRAN is nowhere to be seen.

GORSE: Mo. Hi hi hi hi, Mo. Hi hi hi hi hi, Mo.

MO: *(Stirs.)* Chicky?

GORSE: Chicky here.

MO: Chicky bad?

GORSE: Hi hi, Chicky good, Mo, hi hi, Chicky good.

MO: Hold Chicky.

GORSE: Hi hi hi. *(Reaches for Chicky.)*
Chicky chick chick, hau?

CHICKY: *(Solemnly.)* Fiu prrt fiu prrt fiuuu prrrrt fiiufiufiu.

GORSE: *(Turns MO over.)* Hi hi hi hi hi, Mo.

MO: Oh ah oh.

GORSE: Yeh.

MO: Big animal.

GORSE: Yeh. Yeh. *(Naming the predator.)* Belly biter liver eater.

MO: No belly bite here. We fight.

GORSE: We fight.

MO: *(Indicating her leg.)* Leg biter. I live. Not leg. Leg not live ow.

GORSE: *(Looks at it.)* Yeh, belly-biter bite leg, yeh.

MO: Yeh.

GORSE: Leg live.

MO: Ne.

GORSE: Leg live, Mo.

MO: Leg not live.
Chick chicky chicky chicky chick chick chick chick.
(CHICKY does not come to her.)
Chick chicky chicky chicky chick chick chick chick.
(CHICKY does not come to her.)
Chicky chicky chick chick chick.

GORSE: *(Mutters.)* Piper.

MO: *(Admonishing.)* Gorse.

CHICKY: *(Pulls at grass.)* Fiu prrt fiu prrt fiuuu prrrrt fi-iufiufiu.

A flutter at the periphery.

GORSE: Pah! Dirty birds.

But it's GRAN, high up.

CHICKY: Fiu prrt.

GORSE: Ma!

MO: Gran.

GORSE: How you come there, Ma? Good green grass.

GRAN: I fear. Mo. I not stand with you. I not die with you.

MO: Nay, Gran. Hyeh, hyeh.

GRAN: I old. Old. Heart. Heavy.

MO: Gran.

GRAN: I die; you live, mother.

MO: Ne, Gran.

GORSE: Ma. Ne.

GRAN: One old bad smell here, yeh? I.

CHICKY: Tsa ha tsa dum prreee |
tsa tsee ha prree ha |
(This is derived from a currawong call.)

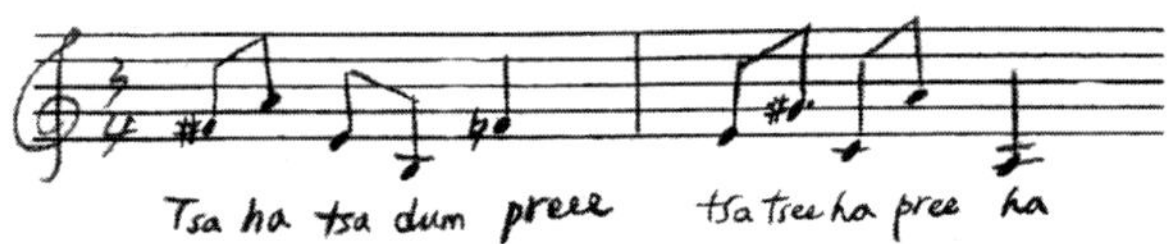

GRAN: Chicky Chicky child.

She comes down to them, looks at MO's leg wound.

GRAN: Bad.

CHICKY: *(Fingers pendant.)* Tsa ha tsa dum prreee |
tsa tsee ha prree ha |

GRAN: *(To GORSE.)* I say, you hear, yes?

GORSE: Yes.

CHICKY: Tsa ha tsa —

GRAN: Hold, Chicky. *(To GORSE.)*
Sharp stone.

GORSE: *(Producing knife.)* Sharp stone.

GRAN: Burn that with fire.

GORSE: Burn this fire.

GRAN: Wipe ashes. Give I.

GORSE: Right.

GRAN: *(To MO.)* Here. Eat salt.

MO: Mmm.

CHICKY: Tsa tsee ha prree ha |

GRAN: Hold, Chicky.

CHICKY: *(Holding out pendant, though it's still around her neck.)*
Tsa ha tsa dum prreee |
tsa tsee ha prree ha |

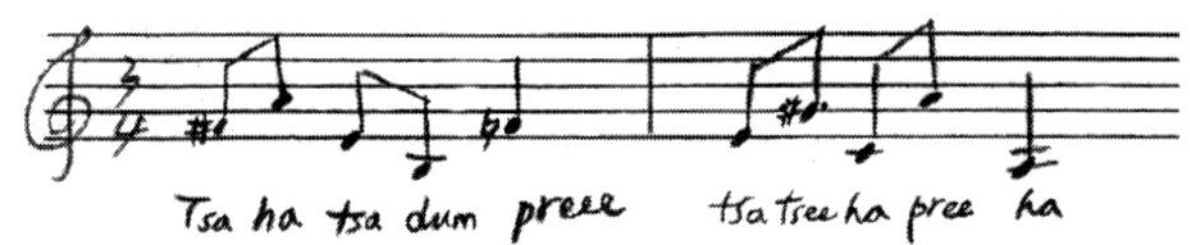

GRAN: What this?

CHICKY pulls the acorn caps apart, exposing the sticky salve within that holds the caps together.

GRAN: Give here.

CHICKY pulls away.

GRAN: Here. I smell.

CHICKY: *(Offers.)* Tsa tsee ha.

GRAN: *(Sniffs.)* Good green guts. You hold this? From pipers, this? What, we rub this in? *(Sniffs.)* We eat this? Ne.

GORSE: Ma.

GRAN: Ne. From pipers, Gorse.

GORSE: From pipers, yeh. She hold that from pipers.

CHICKY: *(Mimes wiping.)*
Tsa tsee ha prree ha |

GRAN: Bah!

GORSE: Ma.

GRAN: From pipers, Gorse. I fear fog in you head.

GORSE: Ma! Chicky hold you heart, yeh.

GRAN: Chicky—

GORSE: Ma! Chicky piper!

GRAN: Good green guts.

GORSE: *(Hand out to Chicky.)* Chicky chick. Here.

CHICKY pulls away.

GORSE: Chicky. Here. You ma bad bite. She not die. Here.

CHICKY pulls away.

GORSE: Here. *(He extends his hand.)*

CHICKY: Fiuuu prrrrt.

GORSE: I hold. *(He puts his hand on the acorn pendant.)*

CHICKY: Fi-iufiufiu.

GORSE: Here. *(He pulls the pendant from around her neck.)*

CHICKY: *(Squats, cries quietly.)* iiiiiiiiiieeeeeeeeeeee. iiiiiiiiieeeeeeeeeee. iiiiiiiiieeeeeeeee.

GORSE: Here, Mo. *(Applies salve.)*

MO: *(Waking.)* Ugh! Good green guts.

GRAN: Uh. Come. Give here. Here. *(Takes the salve.)* Stand there. I wipe this.

GORSE: Good ma.

GRAN: Bah. Pah.

CHICKY: *(Cries quietly.)* iiiiiiiiiieeeeeeeeeeee.

MO: *(As GRAN applies salve.)*

Chicky Chick Chicky Chick — ugh!
Good green guts, Gran. Rotten salt rub. Fire skin, ugh!
Wash.
Water.
Wet.
Woman.
Wash.
Water.
Wet.
Owww!oman.
Good green guts.

Scene Eleven

Night. MO is wrapped up sleeping. GRAN is sitting by her head, nodding off. CHICKY is asleep, a little apart from them. MO is quaking with fever, making little sounds. GORSE is crouching downstage, looking at CHICKY's pendant from all angles. With no salve to hold them together, the two halves have become separated on the leather tie. He examines the tie, holding it up as if about to put it around someone's neck. And then he examines the acorn caps, sniffs them, runs his finger along the closure.

MO's fever grows. Very quietly, A SMALL GROUP OF NEANDERTHALS passes through and exits. No one else sees them save MO. She sits up. Her cries wake GRAN and draw GORSE.

MO: I see you. I see you! Help me! I hate her I hate you!

GRAN: *(MO is speaking gibberish.)* Mo—

MO: What can I say so you'll hear me? Wee Pert? Wee! Pert!

GRAN: I know not what you say, Mo. You say smoke.

MO: Help me! How can I love what I hate TAKE her from me!

GRAN: You say smoke, Mo.

MO: I know where you walk. I know where you WALK.
(To GRAN.) I saw them.

GRAN: Hold, Mo.

MO: I saw them, I know.

Her cries have woken CHICKY, who sits up, makes a tight ball. MO settles.

CHICKY: *(Quietly.)* iiiiiiiiieeeeeeeeeee.

GORSE goes to MO, holding out the pendant to CHICKY.

GORSE: Here, Chicky.

CHICKY: *(Doesn't take it, cries quietly.)* iiiiiieeeee.

GORSE: You hold this. This good. Good fat, this. You good child. Come see, here.

CHICKY: Grr, grr, grrrrrr.

GORSE: See… how you… give... good salt, here.

CHICKY: FrrrooooomoooooowaaaaaaAAAh!

She turns away from him.

GORSE: Oh, Mo. I — *(He thumps his chest, halfhearted, sorry.)*

MO: *(Weak, sleepy.)* Chicky walk back.

GORSE: Chicky what?

MO: Chicky walk back.

GORSE: Chicky walk back where? Here?

MO: Big water. Pipers.

GORSE: Big water? Far water?

MO: Pipers. Chicky know mother blood there. All pipers walk big water. Moon not say why.

GORSE: You Chicky mother. You not die, Mo.

MO: Chicky kill I, Gorse.

GORSE: Chicky ...

MO: Chicky kill I.

GORSE: Nay, Mo: Chicky—

But she rolls over. Goes back to sleep. GORSE comes to front.

GORSE: Moon. My moon. Do you shine on the pipers as much as you shine on the men? You must.

That one is a piper. And yet Mo took her in. There was a moment when I thought we might succeed but now I think we will fail. Look at us. How can we not? And Mo thinks it is her fault but it cannot be her fault. The death of the babe she bore was not her fault. If a piper does not love her it is not her fault. Because this one is a piper. An ignorant piper that does not know what is good for her the way any human child would know. A human child would know what is good for her. You would think any child would know what is good for her. Who else is going to look after her? Who else is going to keep her warm with a fire? Gah!

Maybe she's not even a child maybe she's just a —... How would I know? Piper chicks have faces like ...
like.
like children's faces.
She is a child.
I know she is a child.
Moon.
There is spirit in her fight. She can fight me as much as she likes.
But I wish she would not give Mo such a wound.
When we took in the child, we thought we were doing something to take away Mo's wound.
But then the bear came in the night and tore open the wound, made it bigger, made it for all to see.
And that is really not… *(The word is "just" or "fair.")*
It is not…
IT IS NOT…
(He knocks his head.)
Tell me, Moon, what does this piper expect of us? What does this piper expect of me? You shine on the pipers as much as you shine on the people. How are pipers different from people? We've given her the name Chicky, but I do wonder about the name she might already have.
Like, say:
(Whistles, self-consciously.)
Something like that, you know?

He whistles again, returning to the camp and standing over the sleepers.

Scene Twelve

MO is still in her place, uncovered, now. GRAN is with her. She is manipulating her leg, bending it and straightening it.

MO: Ow.

Elsewhere, GORSE is splitting flint with a rock, surrounded by rejected pieces. CHICKY, becoming curious, picks one up.

GORSE: *(Takes it.)* Sharp, little one. No, little one. Sharp. Here.

He offers her the pendant again. She takes it and flings it away like she did with the meat.

CHICKY: Èh!

GORSE: Oh! No. No no no.

He runs to retrieve it and then places it carefully in a little sack tied around his waist.

MO: Ow.

Meanwhile, CHICKY picks up another piece of flint. She's got a bit of her edge back.

GORSE: No, little one— *(Tries to take it.)*

CHICKY: *(Eludes him.)* Heehaha.

GORSE: Give, Chicky.

CHICKY: Heehooha. *(Slashes his palm open.)*

GORSE: OW!

CHICKY: *(Hopping.)* Heeha heeha heeha. Prrrt.

GORSE: *(Examines palm, ignores CHICKY, pities self.)*
Ow.
Ow, Mo, ow.
Big cut. Good green heavy heart.

CHICKY: *(Hopping.)* oo oo ha ha. Prrt.

GORSE: *(Cups his hurt hand, cradles it in the other.)* Ow-ee.

MO: *(Sighs.)*

GORSE: *(Switch. Looks at CHICKY. Considers. Becomes playfully conspiratorial. Crouches close to her, as the blood pools in his cupped hand.)*
Hold. *(Wait.)*

CHICKY: *(Jumps.)* Heeha.

GORSE: Come see. Here. Come see.

CHICKY: *(Steps closer, looks into his cupped hand.)* Tsee-hee.

GORSE: Blood River water, here, see? Blood River flow. Small Chicky fall in there. See? That you: fight with guts, fight water. *(Swirls, makes wind sound effect.)* Wsshhhh. Blood River pull you in, chick. You not swim, you not float.

CHICKY: Fiu?

GORSE: See? Here: that I. I fear this water. Ugh. I come at Blood River, I fight with guts, fight water. I give you hand. I pull you hand. Two. I, you. You, I. And you laugh: "ahahahaha."

CHICKY: Aha. Aha.

GORSE: Yeh. You laugh, you bite, I cry: ooh hoo, ooh hoo, ha ha!

CHICKY: Ha ha!

MO: Ow.

GORSE: See?

CHICKY: Tsee hee.

GORSE: Ah! Here.
(He dips the index finger of his other hand into the blood.)
See? Hold.
(He paints a line down his own cheek.)
See? I fight with guts, fight water.

CHICKY: Haheeha!
(Trills, whistles, hums, sings.)
Dee-dee dee-dee tee-uwhit.

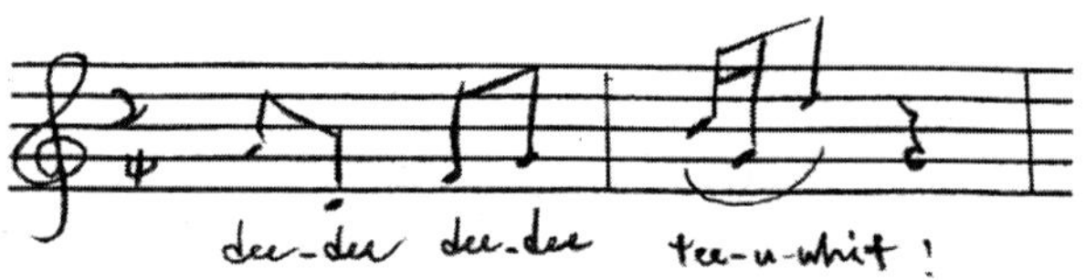

GORSE: You count this good, I see. Hold.

He paints a line down his other cheek.

GORSE: I fight with guts, fight water.

CHICKY: Ha ha! Dee-dee dee-dee tee-uwhit.

GORSE: Sit straight. Here:
(Paints one of her cheeks. He paints the other.)
There. And you fight with guts, fight water.
We fight with guts, fight water.

CHICKY: Dee-dee-dee, dee-dee-dee, dee-dee-dee, tee-uwhit-tu |
tee-uwhit-teeu dee dee—

GORSE: —hahaha

CHICKY: | —tee-uwhit-tu.

Bass clef notes represent accidentally musical hahaha from GORSE. (This is likely derived from common blackbird call.)

GORSE: Yeh.

CHICKY: Yeeha!

GORSE: Yeh.

CHICKY: Yeeha!

GORSE: Come. We hunt: flowers, fruit, leaves, ash and water: red, green, yellow. Come.

CHICKY: Yeeha! Yeeha!

They exit. GRAN is still tending to MO.

GRAN: Stand, Mo.

MO: Yeh. I stand. I stand.

She stands.

MO: I walk.

Walks with a limp but gets it done.

GRAN: Good walk, Mo.

Now we hear GORSE and CHICKY coming; they take a while to enter, finally arriving with their faces painted up in several colours they have found. They are dancing a simple dance in unison, led by CHICKY, rhythmically similar to the way the Neanderthals moved at the start, deliberate like that but more celebratory.

CHICKY: *(Repeating.)* Fti-u ftree, fti-u frtee ti | peet-seet peet-sew fti-u ftee-tree.

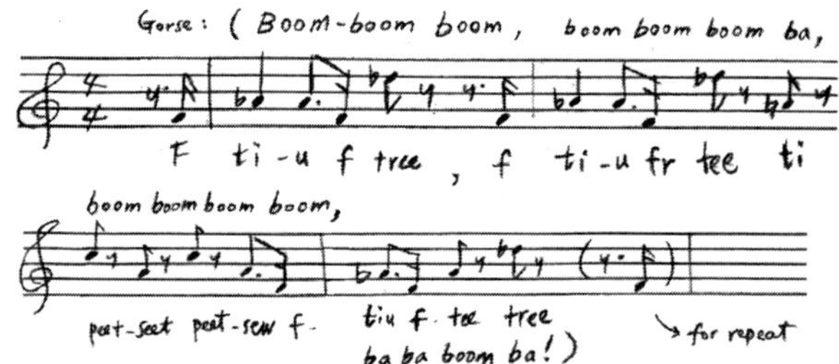

GORSE: *(With CHICKY, repeating.)* Boom-boom boom, boom-boom-boom ba, boom-boom boom boom, ba-ba boom-ba!

GRAN: Good / green grass.

MO: /Good green guts.

GORSE: Yeh. Chicky hold this heart, Mo. This heart hold Chicky. Big heart big day.

MO: Yeh.

GORSE: Big belly day.

MO: Good. Good, Gorse, yeh.

GORSE: And you stand! You walk! See? Good. Chicky. You mama stand, walk.

MO: Gorse.

GORSE: Yeh?

MO: You give think at what I say at night?

GORSE: Huh?

MO: You give think at that?

GORSE: What?

MO: That this child...
(Sighs.)
That this child walk at big water. You give think at that?

GORSE: I... Yeh.

MO: Pipers?

GORSE: Yeh, I... Yeh, I think...

MO: You fear that walk?

GORSE: I... no. I not fear long walk. I...

MO: What?

GORSE: Big water big, Mo. I fear water.

MO: Pah!

GORSE: I fear water, Mo!

MO: Chicky live rotten and die because you fear water?

GORSE: Chicky not die.

MO: With no ma, Chicky die.

GORSE: You Chicky ma. *(Holding up pendant with half-shells.)* This good fat kill bad bite in you leg.

MO: Leg live; I die; Chicky die; you sing and dance and not walk near water.

GORSE: Mo!

MO: Dust.

GORSE: And Gran—

MO: What Gran?

GORSE: Gran not walk long walk, nay. Not good.

MO: *(Turning to GRAN.)* Gran, you fear long walk big water?

GRAN: *(Confused.)* I... no. I not fear long walk big water. I not—

MO: Good. Night come. Sun sleep. Sun come back. We walk.

GORSE: Mo—

MO: You fear that, Gorse?

GORSE: No. W— Yeh; good green guts, Mo.

MO: We walk long road, big water, pipers; she see pipers, she hear pipers, she smell pipers; she know pipers, and, when she know pipers,
(Weighing one hand and other.)
—she stand with pipers,
—she come with us. Yeh? Good.

GRAN: Throw I yellow, yellow heart.

GORSE: Mo. All I know:
—you ma,
—I fa—

MO: Gorse, if Chicky not see pipers, Chicky bite, Chicky fight, Chicky eyes rain, Chicky laugh ahahahaHAHAHEEHA all day, all night, all.

GORSE: I not know.

MO: Chicky rub cold salt in; Chicky kill I, Gorse. I know. We walk.

GORSE: Mo. You live. You ma.

MO: Not ma.

GORSE: You ma!

MO: No!

GORSE: Yes!

MO: Gah!
Gorse.
We go there, we see.

GORSE: We go. We see.

MO: Yeh. *(Shrugs.)* We see.

GORSE: *(Shrugs.)* Sun sleep? Sun come new day? *(i.e., tomorrow.)* We walk?

MO: Sun come new day.

GORSE: Yes?

MO: Yes.

GORSE: We walk?

MO: ... We walk.

GRAN: We walk.

Scene Thirteen

They have prepared their gear. GORSE and CHICKY still have remnants of face paint. GRAN is fussing, uncomfortable, a pain in her side.

GORSE: *(To CHICKY, pointing.)* There. Far. Big water. Pipers. You, me, Ma, Gran, walk. See pipers. Know pipers. You scratch that itch. Not fight. Not bite. Not hit.

GRAN: *(Drops something, picks it up, muttering.)* Belly burn. Ugh. Blood.

MO: *(To CHICKY.)* Chicky. When we walk, far, you know you people; good, yeh?

CHICKY turns away.

MO: *(Stands.)* We walk. Yes? Long road. Big water.

GORSE: We walk.

GRAN: Walk.

GORSE: Big water.

GORSE exits.

MO: Chicky.

CHICKY watches for a moment then runs after GORSE.

MO: Chicky Chick.

GRAN: *(Drops something.)* Skid! Piss! Fug! Spit.

MO, distracted, sighs, follows CHICKY off, still with a limp.

GRAN: Good green guts.

She follows them off, shuffling small steps.

Pause. Then the sound of something large sliding through bush. Swish, swish, swish, swish, swish, swish. The shadow of a large animal — the MAMMOTH — slides across the stage and exits.

Then, as the stage goes to black, we hear a growing cacophony of screeching and barking, predators and carrion-eaters. Just before the stage goes completely black, we see several small shadows moving through, so swift and dark that we cannot tell what they are.

End of Act One.

ACT TWO

Scene One

Night. We hear the sound of the sea. TWO NEANDERTHALS walk through. A YOUNG NEANDERTHAL WOMAN, helping another who is sick. The sick one is singing second half of the mourning phrase from the beginning of the play. Behind them, unseen, we might hear another singing the first half of the phrase.

SICK NEANDER 1: Prrrt... prrt...

Just before they exit, the YOUNG NEANDERTHAL WOMAN helps the SICK ONE to sit. Then she goes back, exits and enters again with ANOTHER SICK NEANDERTHAL, who is singing the first half of the phrase.

SICK NEANDER 2: Fiu/ fiu, fiuuu, fi-iufiufiu.

SICK NEANDER 1: /Prrt. Prrt, prrt.

Perhaps at some point, we see that the YOUNG NEANDERTHAL WOMAN has a CHILD on her back, clinging to her hair. The YOUNG NEANDERTHAL WOMAN helps the first SICK NEANDERTHAL to their feet and they exit all together.

Scene Two

CHICKY, MO, GORSE, GRAN. Everyone is sleeping.

CHICKY: *(In her sleep, laughing.)* Fti-u ftree, ha hee fti-u frtee ti hee hee | peet-seet peet-sew fti-u ftee-tree.

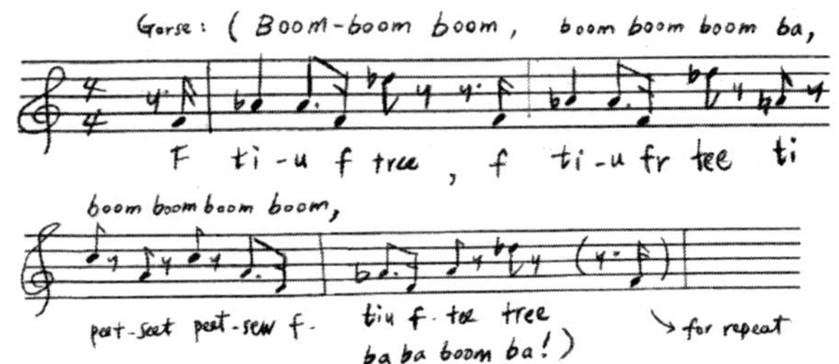

MO: Huh? *(Wakes, rises.)*

CHICKY: *(In her sleep.)* Fti-u ftree, ha hee fti-u frtee ti hee hee —

MO: *(Goes to her.)* Chicky?

CHICKY: *(In her sleep.)* peet-seet heeee peet-sew hooo fti-u ftee-tree.

And she laughs more.

MO: Wha?
You laugh in sleep?
Warm laugh.
You laugh and sing with Gorse in sleep.

Crouches, head down, hand on the sleeping child.

He you da. Gorse you da.
You not stand with pipers, you stand with Gorse.

I you not heart. I.
I not you ma.
Gorse you da.
You sing with Gorse, laugh with Gorse, hunt with Gorse.
You know Gorse. Moon not say why. Who know why. You know Gorse.

You not walk at big water. I pull you at big water. I say, "Come, child, come, see pipers, live with pipers!"
I push you at pipers; I; ugh; nay.
You walk back with Gorse.
You live. You heart. You breathe big. With Gorse.
I walk... I walk...
I wipe this.
I wipe all this.

Lets go, stands, turns away, takes her spear, gathers a few personal belongings and leaves, still with a limp, as the stage goes to black.

Scene Three

Morning. CHICKY wakes, sits up, goes to MO's spot.

CHICKY: *(Crying.)* Hmmmmm; hmmmmm; hmmm-MmmMMMMM!

GORSE: *(Waking.)* What, Chicky?

CHICKY: *(Collapses onto MO's spot, wailing.)* Huhumm-mmmuhhhhh; huhummmmmuhhhh!

GRAN: *(Waking.)* Come here, Chicky. I squeeze you.

GORSE: Mo?
Where Mo?
(Runs off one side and then the other.)
Mo? Mo! Mo!

GRAN: Where Mo, Gorse?

GORSE: *(Returns to CHICKY.)*
Not; not; not not not not not not not; Mo.

GRAN: Oh, Mo.

CHICKY: Hmmmmmmmmm-maa! Hmmm-maa!

GORSE: Wha—?

CHICKY: Hmmmmmmm-mama!

GORSE: Chick chicky chick child. Oh, Mo.

CHICKY: Maaaaa!

GRAN: Chicky child, come. I squeeze you.

CHICKY: *(Turns away.)* Hmmm-ma! Ma? Ma! Mamaa! Ma! Ma.

GRAN: *(Hand out.)* Here. Eat salt.

CHICKY: Hmmmmmmmmmmmmmmmmmaaaaaaa-aaaaaaaa!

GRAN: *(Nods her head, then shakes it.)*
Mo. Hunt Mo.
(Searching the ground.)
Hunt hunt hunt hunt.
(Finds a track.)
Gorse: here.

GORSE: Mo walk?

GRAN: Here. That road.

CHICKY: Hmmmaaa.

GORSE: That one? When she walk, you think?

GRAN: *(Shakes head.)* Sun sleep? With moon?

GORSE: Sun sleep. Mo walk. This road one road, this road two roads, three roads... four roads... five?

GRAN: Many roads.

CHICKY: Hmmmmmmmaaaaaaaaaaaaa!

GORSE: Mo walk many roads. We walk one road. If we hunt Mo, we walk long, not see Mo, not hear Mo, not smell Mo—

GRAN: Dog.

GORSE: Dog ye. Dog hunt Mo. What dog?

GRAN: Dog at Good People.

CHICKY: Hmmmama.

GORSE: Yeh. Good People.

GRAN: You fly that road back to Good People.

GORSE: Neh.
Good People throw fight spit stab push — wash.

GRAN: Not if they not see you.

GORSE: Neh, not if...
If we hunt Mo with dog, Ma, dog come, smell piper, bite Chicky. Dog bite Chicky. Not good. Nay. Good People not We People. Good People not good people: Good People bad people.
Nay. We hold here. Stand. Mo come back.

GRAN: Mo walk river, road, death?

GORSE: Mo come back!

GRAN: I fear.

GORSE: Mo mother, Ma. Mo mother this one here. This child push Mo, pull Mo. Push pull push pull push. And that leg bite cut Mo in head / heart, I not know. Mo heart heavy, and... she walk away.

Mo think she not good mother. Walk away.
Ashes.
Dust; dust; ashes.
Mo good mother, Ma. One mother. Good mother. This child mother.

CHICKY: Mmmmmmmamamaaaaaaaa!

GORSE: .... Hear!
Mo! Hear! Hear! Come back!
We hold here.
Mo come back. This child be Gorse child. Mo child. We hold.

GRAN: We hold.

GORSE: Stand. This not right if Mo not come.

GRAN: Stand.

GORSE: Mo come. One, Mo come. Two, Mo, come. Three, four; five. One-one, two-one, three-one, four-one! Mo come!

GRAN: Mo come.

CHICKY: Mama.

Scene Four

Early morning darkness. We hear a bit of birdsong. MO is sleeping. The birdsong grows in intensity, waking her up. She is a bit bewildered for a moment, doesn't know where she is. She rolls over and then jumps to her feet. All birdsong stops. Silence. She notices. Then one blackbird begins to sing again. She listens intently, looking a bit mad.

MO: Chicky?
No. *(Shakes her head.)*

BLACKBIRD 1: *(Calls.)*

MO listens. Small laugh cut short, stands, listens.

BLACKBIRD 1: *(Calls.)*

BLACKBIRD 2: *(Distant, responds.)*

Smaller laugh cut short to listen harder.

BLACKBIRD 1: *(Calls again.)*

BLACKBIRDS 2,3: *(Distant, overlapping response.)*

MO laughs twice cut short, trying to stop and listen.

BLACKBIRD 4: *(Distant, responds alone.)*

BLACKBIRDS 1,2,3: *(Overlapping response.)*

MO: *(Hysterical laughter.)*

BLACKBIRDS: *(All respond.)*

MO: *(Hysterical laughter, shaking, falling.)*

BLACKBIRDS: *(Cacophony.)*

MO sobs.

BLACKBIRDS die down.

MO sobs alone, stops, gets up, moves on, with more of a limp.

Scene Five

GORSE, GRAN, CHICKY, sunset.

CHICKY: Mama.

GRAN: Sun at foot, Gorse. We sleep.

GORSE: This night I give ear with moon, Ma. I hear what moon say, with this.

CHICKY: Mama.

GRAN: This.

GORSE: Yeh: Mo, and big water; and pipers; and Chicky. All this.

GRAN: And burn fire?

GORSE: You cold, Ma?

GRAN: Yeh.

GORSE: Yeh. Fire.

GORSE gathers sticks, balances them, mouths the counting, CHICKY allows it. When he's got a perfect pile with all the sticks he needs, he looks up, surprised. CHICKY is not paying attention.

CHICKY: Mama.

GORSE: You not kill fire, Chicky?
What, you kill fire when laugh, not when cry yeh. Yeh.

CHICKY: Mama...
(Sings a mourning song. This is derived from a loon call.)
Cooo-leeeeeeeeeeeee-ee.

(Repeats.)
Cooo-leeeeeeeeeeeee-ee.

TWO NEANDERTHALS appear nearby: one is the YOUNG NEANDERTHAL WOMAN we have seen before. She is burying her child, and now we hear her joining CHICKY in the call. GORSE and GRAN do not see where they are but they hear the call. The ADULT NEANDERTHAL makes CHICKY's lonesome call more complex. OTHER NEANDERTHALS answer in the far distance. (This is also derived from a loon call.)

NEANDERS: Cooo-leeeeee-eeee-eeeeee-eeeee-eeeeeee.

The call repeats, overlaps, multiplies. CHICKY is afraid. Buries herself in GORSE.

GORSE: Oh.

GRAN: Oh-oh.

GORSE: They not far.

GRAN: Nay, not far.

GORSE: I smell fear.
They fear.
(To CHICKY.) And you fear.
We walk here to know this? Not big water but here?
To know we with you, you with we? You with Gran, I, Ma, and fear pipers?
This good, yeh? Good salt.
If you fear pipers, that say we not walk big water, ne?
And if you call mama, that say we not walk big water, yeh?

CHICKY: Mama.

GORSE: Ma come back, we walk back. We father, mother, child. Good green grass: This.

GRAN: We walk back? We all walk back?

GORSE: Chicky fear pipers.

GRAN: We walk back. Good people?

GORSE: Ne, Ma, not Good People. We walk back new. Good People not we people.

GRAN: Ne...

GORSE: This child we people.

GRAN: That child You People. You New People.

GORSE: You with we, Ma. We all New People.

GRAN: Ha ha, we all new people. Chicky fear. Chicky say mama. Mo come. We all new people.

GORSE: We walk back.

GRAN: We walk back.
When sun come, Mo come here and we walk back.

GORSE: Why you think Mo come back when sun come, Ma?

GRAN: Because... because this good, Gorse. Because moon give we good salt. Moon not say why. Who know why.
Mo come back, yeh?

GORSE: Yeh.

GORSE sits and listens. CHICKY still won't let go of him. He hears nothing, relaxes and, as the stage goes to black, addresses CHICKY.

GORSE: You fear pipers.
(He is so happy.)
You fear pipers.
Because you with we now. I; Mo; you; people.
You people.
I give salt to moon.

Scene Six

MO. After sunset. She is weak and stumbling. Despairing. There are animals tracking her. THREE HYENAS. We don't see them yet, though we hear them. She slides down her spear.

HYENAS: Hahahahahoohoohooheyaheyaheeheeheeheehahahahoohoo.

MO: Chick chicky chick chick chick chick.

HYENAS: Hahahahahoohoohoo.

MO: Gorse.
Gran.

HYENAS: Hahaheeheeheeheehahahahoohoo.

MO: Ashes. Dust.
How I hear Chicky laugh when animals hunt I? When animals kill I? How I hear Chicky laugh?

HYENAS: Hahahaha.

MO: Turn, Mo. *(Or "Stand, Mo.")*

HYENAS enter, making a wide circle around MO.

HYENAS: Hahahahaheeheehohoheeyaheeyahee!

MO: *(Brandishing spear.)*
Laugh not, Chicky. Fight!

HYENAS: *(Tightening circle.)* Heeheeheeheeheeheeheeheehee.

MO: What you say, Chicky, when you sing at big animal: Come?
(Tries it. Stops. Stands straight. Balls fists. Cries out.)
Brrrrraaa!

HYENAS stop.

MO: *(Stands straighter. Trills loud and slow and low.)*
trrrrrrp, trrrrr-trrr trrrrrp.
trrrrrrp, trrrrr-trrr trr-trrp fug.

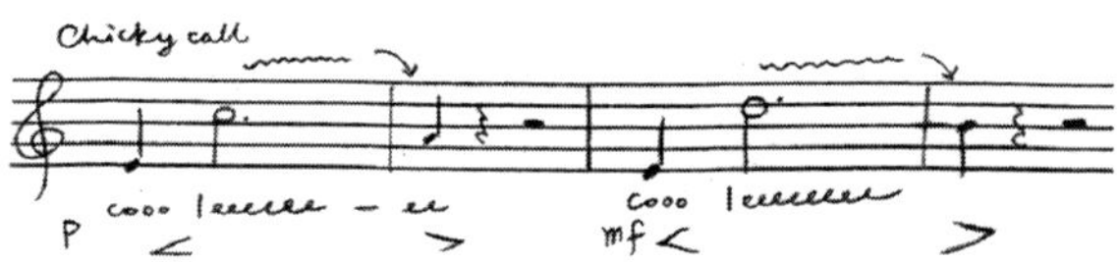

HYENAS: *(Tightening circle.)* Heeheeheeheeheehee-heeheeheehee.

MO: *(Tries again.)* trrrrrrp, trrrrr-trrr trrrrrp—

MAMMOTH: *(Distant, unseen, low rumble, followed by a trumpet.)*
Bgrrrbrgbgrrbbbbrrrrrrrbrrrr, brrgrbbr-bgrrr bgrbgrrr.
Bgrrrbrgbgrrbbbbrrrrrrrbrrrr, brrgrbbr-bgrrr bgrbgrrr-bgrr

HYENAS: *(Widening circle, shocked.)* aa-AAH-ahoh-oh. Euuuuuuugh!

MO: I count that good.

HYENAS: Euuuugh! Euuuugh!

MO: And what she sing all days all nights.

HYENAS: *(Move in.)* Hahahahahaheeheeheehee.

They keep laughing during their coordinated attack.

HYENA 1 snaps.

MO: Fuiprrt! *(Turns, thrusts spear.)*

HYENA 2 snaps at her exposed thigh.

MO: Fuiprrt! *(Turns, thrusts spear, gets low, pulls blade from shin scabbard.)*

HYENA 3 snaps at exposed thigh.

MO: Fiuprrt! *(Stabs back with blade.)*

HYENA 3: *(Hurt.)* aa-AAH-ahoh-oh! *(Runs off.)*

HYENA 1 snaps at spear side as HYENA 2 feints and hesitates.

MO: Prrrrtfiufiufiu! *(Thrusts with spear through HYENA 1.)*

HYENA 1: Euugh. *(Runs off, dying.)* Euuuuuuuuugh!

HYENA 2: *(Hesitates, paces.)* Hahaha. Hahaha. Hahahaha.

MO: What you think?

HYENA 2: Hahaha. Haha. *(Runs off.)*

MO: *(Recovers, sheathes blade, checks wounded thigh, then.)*
Fiu prrt fiu prrt. Fiu prrrrt fi-iufiufiu.

Oh, Chicky. Oh, Chicky.

MO exits.

A moment later she is backed on again, spear raised, tracked by A WOMAN who has no weapon. MO brandishes her spear, threatening.

WOMAN: Careful. Careful. There is no need for that.

MO: What?

WOMAN: Did you not hear me, woman?

MO: You say, I hear, I right not know what you say. Why I know all what you say?

WOMAN: I am the moon.

MO: The moon?

WOMAN: You are a young woman, your time of mourning over, your womb ripe.
But you did not wait.
There is a space of time for mourning decreed by the moon.
You: ended it.
See how you have been punished?
You threw your life away for a piper.

A piper, woman. Here you are, alone in the savage wilderness.
All for the love of a piper.

Do you know the difference between the human and the piper?

Those hums and whistles you have just—hmmmmm-mmimicked.

MO: What they say?

WOMAN: Nothing. There is nothing behind such sounds, nothing within them, no truth to be unlocked; no language. I have cocked my ear to listen, many times, for a hundred thousand years.
Just: wind.

MO: I think not.

WOMAN: *(Touches MO's forehead.)* Pipers Are Animals. They cannot be a part of your family, not even as dogs.

MO: You are wrong.

WOMAN: You have just seen it! Your so-called child laughing through these beasts that sought to eat you.

MO: She was not here.

WOMAN: She would eat you too.

MO: No.

WOMAN: There is nothing there. When she laughs, it is to mimic these cacklers, when she whistles it is to mimic the birds of the air.

MO: Maybe we all found our words that way.

WOMAN: No.

MO: Mimicry and then...

WOMAN: What?

MO: ... longing.

WOMAN: Ha.
Ha!
I am the moon. Nothing happens I do not grant.

MO: That cannot be.

WOMAN: No lightning strike if I am hidden.

MO: Ah! Lightning only strikes when you are hidden.

WOMAN: I am only hidden when—

MO: I was so struck.

WOMAN: You lie.

MO: I have a child—

WOMAN: The moon took your child.

MO: In a lightning strike inspiration, I claimed another child.

WOMAN: I give you words to express anything; you use them to cross me?

MO: I use them to tell the truth.

WOMAN: A quick wit swims in the shallows where it will be speared, eaten and removed from a bloodline that will stretch so far into the future that—

MO: Who's the animal now?

WOMAN: I sew smart mouths shut.

MO: If I have a smart mouth, I must thank myself it seems and not the moon.

WOMAN: I will show you the power of the moon.
(She gestures a sound of laughing men.)
I will rape you and leave you a heifer, a crow, a tree, a stone—

MO: I had a family.

WOMAN: But I promise your womb will bring forth a race of perfect men, who will travel to the sea and kill the last of that kind like your ignorant—

MO screams.

WOMAN: —piper. *(She grabs MO by the throat.)*

MO: Die,god. *(Hoarse.)*

WOMAN falters.

MO: Die, god. Die, god. Die, god! *(Repeat as long as it takes for the moon to collapse and die.)*
I say. Moon not say.
Moon not say; I say.
Moon not know why. I know why.
(To corpse.) Hear this, god-dust; hear this, god-ashes:
You know never what I know. You know never what I think.
I mother that child.
I. Mother. that child.
Chicky bite I,
Chicky push I,
Chicky spit I.
Chicky fight I,
Chicky kill I.
Chicky know I.
Chicky know I.
I mother that child Chicky; I mother.

Exits.

Scene Seven

GRAN wakes at first light. There is fog. She goes to GORSE, who is contemplating the sleeping CHICKY. He has the pendant out, looking at it, too, as it dangles from his fingers.

GRAN: Chicky sleep good, Gorse.
This day, Mo come, we walk back, yeah.

GORSE: Ma.

GRAN: You give ear with moon at night? You think with moon?

GORSE: Ne. Clouds come. No moon all night. I think with I. With Chicky.

GRAN: Oh.

GORSE: All night, I smell fear, Ma. Piper fear. Chicky fear. Fear-smell here, there, sky, earth. Fear. They fear we. And Chicky fear they. Nay? Not good.
Not good.
Good green guts.
Ma:
If Chicky fear they, Chicky fear all pipers; if Chicky fear all pipers, Chicky fear to live. Chicky fear Chicky.
(To the sleeping CHICKY.) You fear you.
And if you fear you, you fear I, Mo, Gran, all.
You fear to live.
Nay... nay... nay...
This day, Ma, Chicky come to know.
And I come to know.
We come to know.

GRAN: Know… what?

GORSE: Gran… Chicky and I walk.

GRAN: Walk… where?

GORSE: Pipers. Big water.

GRAN: You and Chicky… walk big water.

GORSE: Yeh. And pipers.
This people here—piper people—hold chicky blood, chicky heart, chicky eyes. I not fear them. Chicky see now I not fear them. Chicky not fear them, Chicky not fear Chicky. If I good father, I kill fear in Chicky.
This how I kill fear in Chicky.

GRAN: Pipers. Big water.

GORSE: Pipers. Big water.

GRAN: Who come?

GORSE: Chicky, I.

GRAN: And I.

GORSE: Not you. You hold here, Ma, here when Mo walk back.

GRAN: I come!

GORSE: Nay.

GRAN: I come with you, Gorse.

GORSE: Ma.

GRAN: Gorse.

GORSE: Mo.

GRAN: I die here, Gorse.

GORSE: Nay. I come back.

GRAN: Not if you die. If you die, you not come back.

GORSE: I not die.

GRAN: And if Chicky stand with pipers, Chicky not come back…

GORSE: Neh, Gran. Chicky come back, Chicky not stand with—

GRAN: Gorse!
If you walk big water with Chicky, and if Chicky see pipers, hear pipers, know pipers, walk to hold pipers, she stand with pipers and you give Chicky that.

GORSE: Gran—

GRAN: Gorse! That why you come here! You give Chicky that.

GORSE: Yeh, Ma… yeh… And if Chicky stand with pipers—

GRAN: —I not see her if I here, I not hold her if I here. I come with you, Gorse.

His silence gives assent.

GORSE: *(Waking CHICKY.)*
Chicky. Chicky. Big piper child.
We walk big water, yeh? We walk big water.

CHICKY: Fiu prrt.

He goes, with CHICKY. GRAN is alone for a moment.

GRAN: You come here, Mo. You come here and… sit.
You sit. Here.
You Chicky mother. And...
I you mother, Mo. I mother you.

She tries to fashion a clear place to sit as a message to MO. The effort causes a pain in her liver.

Oh!
Sit here, Mo. And we come back.

She goes, clutching her belly.

Scene Eight

The sound of the sea. GORSE and GRAN and CHICKY are looking down from a high bluff with little pink flowers. GORSE and GRAN discuss what they see. CHICKY just stands and stares, standing very still. We might hear, in the distance, the song of THE NEANDERTHALS walking into the sea from the end of the scene.

GRAN: Many pipers.

GORSE: Yeh. Many.
They cold. You cold?

GRAN: Ne.

GORSE: They cold.
They fall heavy.
They all fall heavy. Stand. Fall. Stand.

CHICKY: *(Staring down at them.)* Fiu prrt.

GORSE: They not good, Ma. Skin bad. Belly swell.
See? *(Gasps.)*
That one die.

GRAN: Where?

GORSE: There. He lie. Not stand...
That one die, Ma.
Oh, I fear they.
(Covers his mouth, looks at CHICKY.)
Nay. I not fear they.
Where they all walk? That big water there.

GRAN: They walk at big salt water.

GORSE: Ne— Big salt water pull you in, Ma. You not swim, you not float.
Big water kill you.

GRAN: Big water kill you, Gorse.

GORSE: Yeh. I fear water.

GRAN: Not they.

GORSE: They swim? All they?

GRAN shrugs.

GORSE: What for?

GRAN: When cold come, when snow come, birds fly far earth.

GORSE: Birds fly, yeh. They not fly, Ma.

GRAN: Swim.

GORSE: Not one man swim far earth. Not one. All suck in water, die. They not fish.

GRAN: Nay, they not fish.

GORSE: Why they walk there?

GRAN: Moon not say why. Who know why.

GORSE: Nay.
I fear this water.
Hold.
See there! *(Points.)*
I see one... two... three, four, five.
They walk in water, swim, five.

And when they swim far, I count one two three four five walk in water, swim.

GRAN: And... If we give they Chicky... Chicky swim with they? They hold Chicky in water this day?

GORSE: Neh.

CHICKY: *(Still staring.)* Fiu prrt.

GORSE: Not all swim, I think, neh. Some pipers stand there, see? We walk at they, nay? They that stand?

GRAN: Because Chicky not swim. Chicky breathe water, die.

GORSE: Yeh.

GRAN: Yeh.

We hear a chant from THE NEANDERTHALS to match the sound of the sea that they are entering. Song a variation of the loon call by way of humpback whale.

NEANDERS: cooo-leeee… cooo-leeee… cooo-leeee…

Scene Nine

All goes quiet. In the dark we hear CHICKY. (This is derived from the last-known call of a Kaua'i 'ō'ō bird.)

CHICKY: kee too ka | ka ta kedooloo too |

She is saying, "No one will say my name." The lights come up and we see CHICKY alone. Then the sounds come back one by one. GORSE appears behind CHICKY, GRAN behind GORSE. Several Neanderthals appear, chanting an aggressive song to drive the humans away. (This song is derived from an extant recording of an ivory-billed woodpecker.)

NEANDERS: a-ha a-ha
uk uk | uk
ee a-ha a-ha |
a-ha- | -a a-ha lee
a-ha | a-ha
uk uk uk |
ee a-ha a-ha.

Some of THE NEANDERTHALS are dressed in the feathered regalia. They are afraid. They look sick and worried. They have sores on their skin. As they chant, a YOUNG NEANDERTHAL WOMAN appears, steps forward until she is in front of CHICKY. She is the YOUNG NEANDERTHAL WOMAN we have seen before. ONE MAN hovers behind the WOMAN. CHICKY cowers behind GORSE, who is muttering his own version of their chant back at them.

GORSE: Throw fight spit stab push, wash; throw fight spit stab push, wash.

The YOUNG WOMAN has a pendant around her neck just like CHICKY's, with the salve. She goes down on one knee, extends her hand towards CHICKY. Is about to speak. But there is still the cacophony from THE NEANDERTHALS. So she turns and addresses them.

N. WOMAN: Aiiieeeeeeeee! iieeeaa!

They stop their chant. The YOUNG WOMAN returns her attention to CHICKY.

N. WOMAN: Prrreeee ee pree-ee-eeeeeee, trrr-rrr?

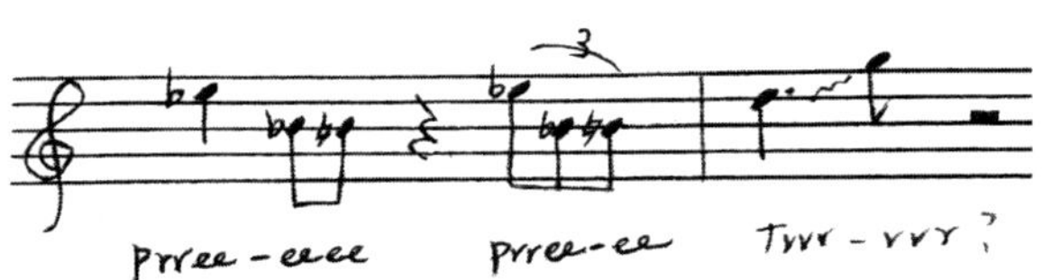

GORSE: What she say?

GRAN: I think she say: "What you name?"

N. WOMAN: Prrreeee ee pree-ee-eeeeeee, trrr-rrr?

GRAN: "What you name, child?"

GORSE: You think she not know Chicky?

GRAN: See with you eyes, Gorse: Chicky not know this woman.

The YOUNG WOMAN focusses on CHICKY, holding out her hands.

N. WOMAN: Trrr-rrr?

CHICKY: *(Still behind GORSE.)* Szzt-mm-muwu-mu(mu)-muwu-mu(mu)-weeuweet. *(This is derived from a humpback whale call.)*

The YOUNG NEANDERTHAL WOMAN nods.

GORSE: Wha?

N. WOMAN: Szzt-mm-muwu-mu(mu)-muwu-mu(mu)-weeuweet.

GRAN: Chicky name, Gorse.

GORSE: Yeh, Ma, I know.

CHICKY steps out from behind GORSE, takes the space between him and the YOUNG NEANDERTHAL WOMAN. GORSE makes to snatch her back but relents at the last moment.

The YOUNG NEANDERTHAL WOMAN speaks to CHICKY, holding out her hand.

N. WOMAN: wheep wheep | kleet hee-eer he-eer | wheep wheep here | fee- der-de
rrt | heer dee dee heer dee dee rrt rrt | rrt rrt | heer dee dee heer dee dee rrt | rrt |

CHICKY steps forward, takes the YOUNG NEANDERTHAL WOMAN's hand, the YOUNG NEANDERTHAL WOMAN embraces her.

GRAN: Oh!

GORSE: Erg.

GRAN: You not give they Chicky, Gorse!

GORSE: You say I give Chicky this, Ma!

GRAN: You give Chicky this, Gorse. But not give they Chicky!

GORSE: Nay, I not give they Chicky.

GRAN: Hi hi hi hi.

GORSE: And if Chicky know what good for Chicky…

GRAN: You not give Chicky.

GORSE: Ma! Chicky give Chicky!

NEANDERTHALS briefly resume their aggressive chant, startling GORSE back to his task.

GRAN: Hi hi hi hi.

GORSE: Hi hi hi hi.
Yeh… yeh… and I say…
(To the YOUNG NEANDERTHAL WOMAN.)
I hold right hand heart.
I hold left hand you.
I not fight you.
I know child. I come here to know you with Chicky.
I come here with that in head, yeh, and...
Here you see Chicky father. You not see mother. Mother not here.
And that… uh…

GRAN: She see father. Father good.

GORSE: Where Mo, Ma?

GRAN: Not this now, Gorse.

GORSE: I all fog with no Mo, Ma. Where Mo? Mo walk back Good People?
Mo dust? Mo ashes?

GRAN: You father, Gorse. You good father. Say.

GORSE: I say.

(Back out to THE NEANDERTHALS.)

I stand with Chicky;
I say you:
Chicky say "home" when she eat: homehomehomehomehomehome.

And… When I with Chicky? I home!
When I with that child? I home!
Father; mother; child; home.
Here home if I with that child here!
Here home, and…
Yeh, and what for you here, at big water? What for? I not see what for and that...
I fear that.

N. WOMAN: *(To GORSE.)* Prrreeee ee pree-ee-eeeeeee, trrr-rrr?

GRAN: She ask you—

GORSE: Yeh, you ask name, yeh. Gorse. I Gorse. I Chicky fa. Chicky father.

There are sticks scattered around. GORSE gathers them, addresses CHICKY.

Oh, I know.
See sticks, Chicky?
I count sticks!
(Balancing three sticks.)
Stick one! stick two! stick three...
There.

CHICKY: *(Small laugh.)* Heha.

GORSE: Yeh; yeh; I hear that. Heart swell.
(Takes more sticks; he playfully performs his old counting confusion.)
Stick four, Chicky! ... Stick five...
Stick two-one. Ne.
Nay! I know this, Chicky! I know!
(Resumes.)
Stick one-one... Stick one-two... stick one-three—

CHICKY: *(Breaks away from WOMAN, runs through the sticks.)*
Heeheeheeheeheeheehahaha.

YOUNG NEANDERTHAL WOMAN cries out, runs to stop CHICKY, misses, holds back.

Her cry frightens THE NEANDERTHALS, who resume their chant. This in turn frightens CHICKY, who is afraid now to go to GORSE or the YOUNG NEANDERTHAL WOMAN. She's alone again.

NEANDERS: *(Chaotic, not in unison.)*
a-ha a-ha uk uk | uk ee a-ha a-ha.

MO: *(Unseen.)* Fiu prrt fiu prrt. Fiu fiuu prrrrt fi-iufiufiu!

GORSE: Mo.
Hold.

MO: *(Appears, calling CHICKY's standard song.)*
Fiu prrt fiu prrt. Fiu fiuu prrrrt fi-iufiufiu.

NEANDERS: *(Quietly gossiping out of sync under what follows.)*
a-ha a-ha uk uk | uk ee a-ha a-ha.

CHICKY: *(To MO.)* Fiu prrt fiu prrt. Fiu prrrrt fi-iufiufiu.

GORSE: You know what she say when she sing that?

MO: Nay, Gorse.

GORSE: Nay?

MO: Nay!

N. WOMAN: *(More gently calling for attention.)* Aiiieeeee-eeee! iieeeaa!

(Then.) Fiu prrt fiu prrt. Fiu prrrrt fi-iufiufiu.

Then she sings CHICKY's line again, in the more stately style from the dying adults at the top of the play. As she sings, she performs its meaning.

N. WOMAN: fiu

One hand over heart, other hand over stomach, she sags, "sick." Perhaps she repeats this until MO gets something from it.

MO: Bad.

GRAN: *(Nodding, her hand on her own belly.)* Bad.

N. WOMAN: prrt

She gestures forward and then deliberately steps forward, "all day." Repeats it.

MO: *(Trying the gesture.)* All Day.

N. WOMAN: fiu

One hand over heart, other hand over stomach, she sags, "sick."

GORSE: *(Trying the gesture, too.)* Bad.

N. WOMAN: prrt

She gestures forward and then deliberately steps forward, "all night."

GORSE: All Night.

N. WOMAN: fiu

Back to sick gesture, she drops to one knee, "dying."

MO: Die come.

N. WOMAN: prrrrrt

Holds her hand up open and the one finger, "wait."

MO: Stand. Hold.

N. WOMAN: fiufiufiu

Falls "dead."

GORSE: Die.

N. WOMAN: *(Rises, puts it all together.)* Fiu prrt fiu prrt. Fiu prrrrt fi-iufiufiu.

MO: Bad. All Day. Bad. All Night. Die come. Stand. Hold. Die.

CHICKY lets go of the YOUNG NEANDERTHAL WOMAN's hand, steps closer to MO. She is between them. Nobody moves. A NEANDERTHAL MAN speaks to the YOUNG WOMAN, CHICKY is not distracted from MO.

MO: *(To CHICKY.)* I think I see. /

The TWO NEANDERTHALS argue—high and low, overlapping MO.

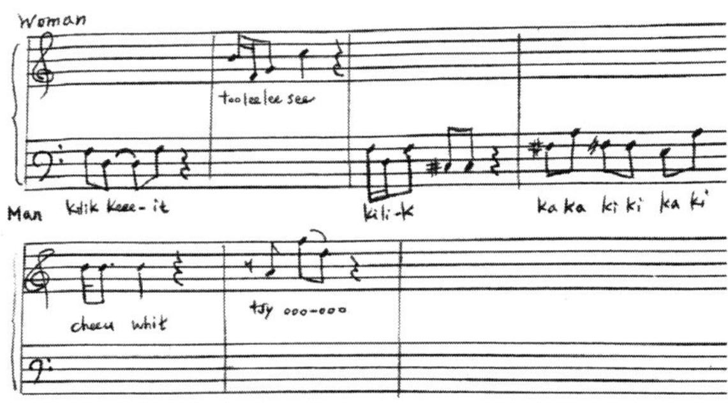

MO: *(To CHICKY.)* You sing how you die. / MAN: killik keeeeee-it.

All day, all night / WOMAN: too-lee-lee see

when you live with we / MAN: killik ka-ka |

you sing how you all die / MAN: ka-ka jop ki-ki-ki-ka-ki |

fiu prrt— *(Interrupted.)* WOMAN: chee-u-whit tsyoooooo/ooo

MAN: *killik keeeeee-it. killik keeeeee—*

CHICKY: *(Who has heard everything.)* Aiieeeeeeeeeeeeeeeeeeeeeeeeeeeeeeeee-yeh!

She turns to MO, who is there, gestures.

CHICKY: kee too ka | ka ta kedooloo too |

MO: I know not what you sing.

CHICKY: *(Pointing at her, she is saying, "No one will say my name.")*

kee too ka: ka ta kedooloo too?

MO: I ... know not what you sing.
I hold right hand heart,
I hold left hand you:
I hold you all days. All days. Moon not know this. I know this.

CHICKY: *(Turns back to the YOUNG NEANDERTHAL WOMAN, speaks to her, gesturing back to MO.)* Zzt trrr-rrr?

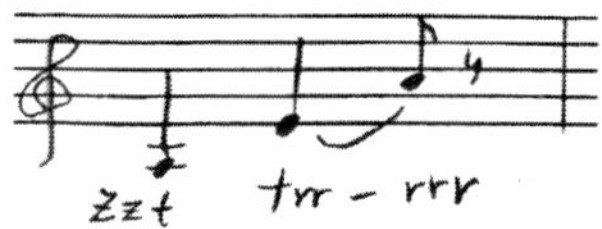

YOUNG NEANDERTHAL WOMAN nods. She steps forward, addresses MO.

N. WOMAN: Prrreeee ee pree-ee-eeeeeee, trrr-rrr?

MO: What?

GORSE appears now too, on the MO side.

GORSE: She say: What name you?

MO: You know this?

GORSE: Yeh, Mo. I know piper tongue.

MO: Gorse.
(Addressing YOUNG WOMAN.) I Mo. Mo.
I Chicky mother.

The YOUNG NEANDERTHAL WOMAN reaches out to CHICKY with one hand and makes a gesture with her other hand held out and open to MO.

N. WOMAN: Szzt-mm-muwu-mu(mu)-muwu-mu(mu)-weeuweet.

GORSE: She say Chicky name. That Chicky name.

MO: Yes.
And I say Chicky name, yes?
I say, I sing, Chicky name. Yes.

GORSE nods.

MO: *(MO tries to say the child's name.)* Zzzt-t-d-nnnnnwweet.

CHICKY doesn't move.

MO: …

GORSE: Mo—

MO: …

GORSE: Mo, you sing Chicky name.

MO: Yeh, Gorse, yeh! I think. Shu!

(She tries again, increasingly loud and desperate.)
Szzzt-t-t-mmmmmmwweewt.
Szzzt-t-t-mmmmmmwweewt!
Szzt-mm-muwu-mu(mu)-muwu-mu(mu)-weeuweet!

As if in response to this, the NEANDERTHAL MAN turns away from them and, calling "chee-u-whit tsyoooooo/ooo!" he resumes the walk into the sea. The others follow suit, joining him in the call and resuming their measured walk into the sea. Song a variation of the loon call by way of humpback whale.

NEANDERS: cooo-leeee… cooo-leeee… cooo-leeee…

N. WOMAN: *(Who needs more time.)* iieeeaa!

But they go on. CHICKY, afraid, comes to MO, looking out towards the sea. The YOUNG NEANDERTHAL WOMAN turns to go.

CHICKY: Èh! Èh!

The YOUNG NEANDERTHAL WOMAN turns back to CHICKY and then turns to go, reaching the water amid the sound of the waves and the fading song of THE NEANDERTHALS.

MO: What come here? What bad come here?

GORSE: They not swim. They die.

CHICKY reaches out, calling and whistling.

CHICKY: Cooo-leeeeeeeeeeeee-ee.

GORSE: Moon pull they in.

MO: Pah.

CHICKY pulls away from MO, runs to the edge of the water.

MO: No!

CHICKY: Èh! Èh!

GORSE: Chicky!

CHICKY turns, confused and lost, GORSE runs his finger down his cheek.

GORSE: You fight with guts, fight water, Chicky. Fight with guts, fight water!

CHICKY: *(Reaching towards the YOUNG NEANDERTHAL WOMAN, she runs her finger down her cheek over and over again with both hands, she speaks in the slow tongue.)*
FI WI GUH FI WAH
FI! WI! GUH! FI! WAH!
FI! WI! GUH! FI! WAAH!
Waaaaaaah!

N. WOMAN: *(Having waded into the water, she has not been able to go. She turns to look at MO and GORSE and CHICKY.)*

Cooo-leeeeee-eeee-eeeeee-eeeee-eeeeeee.

GRAN approaches her, reaches out to her with her hand up.

GRAN: Here, woman, here; eat salt. Ah.

GRAN falls, the YOUNG NEANDERTHAL WOMAN raises her hand and GRAN catches hold of it. Now the YOUNG NEANDERTHAL WOMAN has a problem. She looks back towards MO and GORSE and CHICKY. The sounds of THE NEANDERTHALS are gone, leaving only the sound of the surf. MO holds CHICKY while GORSE steps forward to help. GORSE brings her back, but GRAN has taken the YOUNG NEANDERTHAL WOMAN's hand and will not let go, so she must come too. They bring GRAN back to the others. When they get there, CHICKY embraces GRAN.

GRAN: You squeeze me. You squeeze me.

MO: We all squeeze you, Gran.

GRAN: Mo: Chicky here. She say, "mama." When you walk far. She say it.

GORSE: She say it, Mo.

MO: Yeh, I know.

GRAN: *(Now to the YOUNG NEANDERTHAL WOMAN, still in CHICKY's embrace.)*
And you. Piper Woman. You fight. You live. Chicky hold you in hand.
You sing. You speak. You know. We not know what you know. If Chicky live, you live. If you live, Chicky live.

After a moment, the YOUNG NEANDERTHAL WOMAN nods.

GRAN: We people. We New People.

Blackout. The sound of the waves recedes.

Scene Ten

The stage is empty but for shadows of trees, dead leaves and undergrowth. There is a flutter of carrion wings on the periphery.

HIDDEN HEDGEHOG: *(Barely audible.)* tt, t, t, t, t, t,t .

The YOUNG NEANDERTHAL WOMAN leaps in, spear in hand.

N. WOMAN: Aiiieeeeeeeee!

She kills the HIDDEN HEDGEHOG. CHICKY enters.

CHICKY: Haheeha!
(Trills, whistles, hums, sings.)
Dee-dee dee-dee tee-uwhit.

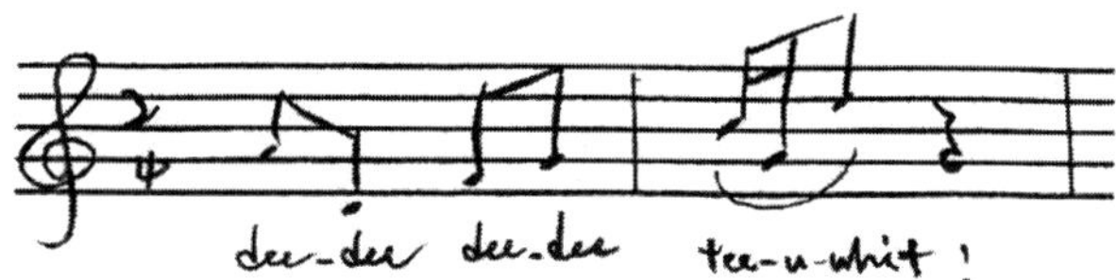

N. WOMAN: Ta tsa-ha-dum twee du-hum |

The two of them withdraw just as GORSE appears.

GORSE: Oh! Birds. Hold. Who hunts with you?

Withdraws as CHICKY puts her finger to her lips.

CHICKY: Shhhhhh.

The stage is empty. A CARRION BIRD enters to investigate the kill. Then A SECOND. The birds are drawn in.

CARRION: Krrrk. Kwak.

MO appears from one side of the stage and the YOUNG NEANDERTHAL WOMAN appears from the other.

N. WOMAN: rrrrrrrrrrrrrrrrrrrrrrrriii!

MO: / eeeeeeeeeeyeeyah!

They kill THE BIRDS. Sit down to pluck feathers.

N. WOMAN: Ta tsa-ha-dum twee du-hum—

MO: *(Doing her best.)*
Ta tsa-ha-dum twee du-hum—

CHICKY: *(Joining in unison with YOUNG NEANDERTHAL WOMAN, getting excited.)*
taa twee duhm- |
-um twee-dum | tsa-hee-ha-doo |

MO: taa twee duhm

N. WOMAN:/
CHICKY: *(MO, echoing.)*
-um twee-dum | tsa-hee-ha-doo |
tsa ha tse dee | -

Lights fade.

The end.

Approximate Neanderthal phrase translations:

Fiu prrt fiu prrrrrrt fiu prrrt fi-iufiufiu.
"Sick, all day, sick, all night, dying, wait, death."
Pied Butcherbird.

Ete oto ete pee-yoo-tsay pee-yoo- tsay | Ete oto ete pee-yoo-tsay pee-yoo-tsay | Ete oto ete pee-yoo-tsay?
"I'm eating, it's good, it's really good, I'm eating, feels good."

Dee-dee dee-dee tee-uwhit
"Play with me!" (Or: "You're playing with me!" Or, "We're playing!")
Common Blackbird.

Ta tsa-ha-dum twee du-hum | taa twee duhm | um twee-dum | tsa-hee-ha-doo | tsa ha tse dee | -tsee ha-doo.
"Sneak up on birds, sneak, sneak up on eating birds, take birds, take feathers, take flight."
Hermit thrush.

Tsa, ha tsa dum preee
tsa, tsee ha pree ha

"This is a help thing. This makes better."
Currawong.

Dee-dee-dee, dee-dee-dee, dee-dee-dee, tee-uwhit-tu | tee-uwhit-teeu dee dee ... | ... tee-uwhit-tu.
"Playing, we're playing, you play with me, playing we, we play," etc.
Common Blackbird.

fti-u ftree, fti-u frtee, ti | peet-seet peet-sew fti-u ftee-tree.
Nonsense that's all variations of 'play':
like saying : play, peelay, waypay, kay, cray, play.
Pied Butcherbird.

a-ha a-ha
uk uk | uk
ee a-ha a-ha | a-ha- | -a a-ha lee
a-ha | a-ha uk uk uk | ee a-ha a-ha.
"Drive them out DRIVE THEM AWAY drive them out and away."
Ivory-billed woodpecker.

wheep wheep | kleet hee-eer he-eer | wheep wheep here | fee- der-de
| fvv rrt dee dee | heer dee dee rrt rrt |
—-rrt dee dee | heer dee dee rrt rrt |
"I'm sad to be without you, Look at me I'm just like your mother, won't hurt you,
Come to me, come to me, come to me."
Pied Butcherbird.

(The two Neanderthals argue — high and low — humpback whale.)

killik keeeeee-it.
"Take her back."

too-lee-lee see
"Let her play."

killik ka-ka |
"Drive them away."

ka-ka jop ki-ki-ḳi-ka-ki |
"Make them go and kill them."

chee-u-whit tsyoooooo/ooo |
"Let us leave them be."

killik keeeeee-it. killik keeeeee—(interrupted)
"Take her back, take her— "

Prrreeee ee i-rrrrrrrr pree-ee-eeeeeee, trrr-rrr?
"What is your name?"

Zzt trrr-rrr?
"Help with my name."
(This is the first note of Chicky's real name plus the last note of the "what is your name" phrase.)

Szzt-mm-muwu-mu(mu)-muwu-mu(mu)-weeuweet!
"Chicky's name."
Humpback whale.

kee too ka | ka ta kedooloo too |

"No one will say my name."
Last-known call of a Kaua'i 'ō'ō bird.

Swadesh List

ALL
AND
ANIMAL
ASHES
AT

BACK
BAD
BARK (OF A TREE)
BECAUSE
BELLY
BIG
BIRD
TO BITE
BLACK
BLOOD
TO BLOW (WIND)
BONE
TO BREATHE
TO BURN (INTRANS.)

CHILD (YOUNG)
CLOUD
COLD (WEATHER)
TO COME
TO COUNT
TO CUT

DAY (NOT NIGHT)
TO DIE
TO DIG
DIRTY
DOG
TO DRINK
DRY (SUBSTANCE)
DULL (KNIFE)
DUST

EAR
EARTH (SOIL)
TO EAT
EGG
EYE

TO FALL (DROP)
FAR
FAT (SUBSTANCE)
FATHER
TO FEAR
FEATHER (LARGE)
FEW
TO FIGHT
FIRE
FISH
FIVE
TO FLOAT
TO FLOW
FLOWER
TO FLY
FOG

FOOT
FOUR
TO FREEZE
FRUIT

TO GIVE
GOOD
GRASS
GREEN
GUTS

HAIR
HAND
HE
HEAD
TO HEAR
HEART
HEAVY
HERE
TO HIT
HOLD (IN HAND)
HOW
TO HUNT (GAME)
HUSBAND

I
ICE
IF
IN

TO KILL
KNOW (FACTS)

LAKE
TO LAUGH
LEAF
LEFT (HAND)
LEG
TO LIE (ON SIDE)
TO LIVE
LIVER
LONG
LOUSE

MAN (MALE)
MANY
MEAT (FLESH)
MOON
MOTHER
MOUNTAIN
MOUTH

NAME
NARROW
NEAR
NECK
NEW
NIGHT
NOSE
NOT
OLD
ONE
OTHER

PERSON
TO PLAY
TO PULL
TO PUSH

TO RAIN
RED
RIGHT (CORRECT)
RIGHT (HAND)
RIVER
ROAD
ROOT
ROPE
ROTTEN (LOG)
RUB

SALT
SAND
TO SAY
SCRATCH (ITCH)
SEA (OCEAN)
TO SEE
SEED
TO SEW
SHARP (KNIFE)
SHORT
TO SING
TO SIT
SKIN (OF PERSON)
SKY
TO SLEEP
SMALL
TO SMELL (PERCEIVE)
SMOKE
SMOOTH
SNAKE
SNOW
SOME
TO SPIT
TO SPLIT
TO SQUEEZE
TO STAB (OR STICK)
TO STAND
STAR
STICK (OF WOOD)
STONE
STRAIGHT
TO SUCK
SUN
TO SWELL
TO SWIM

TAIL
THAT
THERE
THEY
THICK
THIN
TO THINK
THIS
THOU / YOU
THREE
TO THROW
TO TIE
TONGUE
TOOTH (FRONT)
TREE
TO TURN (VEER)
TWO

TO VOMIT

TO WALK
WARM (WEATHER)
TO WASH
WATER
WE
WET
WHAT
WHEN
WHERE
WHITE
WHO
WIDE
WIFE
WIND (BREEZE)
WING
WIPE
WITH (ACCOMP)
WOMAN
WOODS
WORM

YE
YEAR
YELLOW

The Inspiration for *Orphan Song*

In 2014, my wife and I adopted a 13-month old girl. I'm going to call her LRD, short for "Little Red Dot," which is how we refer to her on social media, due to the coat she was wearing in the photo in which she first got carried into our house.

Among the books I read to LRD in those first few months, there was one called *Little Gorilla*.

It concerned a baby gorilla who was beloved of everyone in the forest—mother, father, grandma, grandpa, aunts, uncles: "Even when he was only one day old, everybody loved Little Gorilla."

Regard for this baby gorilla extended beyond the gorilla clan to include butterflies, parrots, monkeys, boa constrictors, giraffes, a pair of elephants young and old, a lion, and a hippo.

But then the story takes a turn because the little gorilla starts to grow, and we're supposed to get an ominous feeling about this because the book stops showing him for a few pages. It just shows all the other animals looking at him while he's offstage. He grows and grows, and then the book finally shows him filling up two pages and looking very much like an ashamed full-size gorilla.

So then all the animals come, and you think they're going to tell him that he has to leave the forest.

But they don't do that. They all get together with a cake and some candles and they shout, "Happy birthday, Little Gorilla!"

And the book ends with a picture of Little Gorilla's smiling face and the line, "And everybody still loved him."

The first time I read that book to LRD, she was about 15 months old. When I got to the line, "And everybody still loved him," she shook her head and said, "No."

So. I thought maybe I had heard wrong so I flipped back a few pages and read the last part of the book again. And when I got to the last page, after the birthday, and read the line, "And everybody still loved him," she shook her head and said, "No."

Adopted children remember the people who (from their point of view) have abandoned them. All current models of adoption grapple with this problem and have created certain strategies for dealing with it: primarily openness to the birth family and/or foster parents. This is not an easy thing for adoptive parents to do, especially at a time when they haven't firmly established their own attachment and authority. It's frightening. In our case, when we would make early visits to the foster home, LRD would not want to leave with us at the end of the visit. If they visited our home, she would expect to leave with them at the end.

This little anecdote about the foster visits might make it seem like the needs of the parent and the needs of the child are at odds. But it's of paramount importance for parents to be fearless about prioritizing the needs of the child. We were always told that the fact of LRD feeling attached to her foster parents was a good thing. It meant that she had not given up on the idea of people loving her (as some babies do,) and that she would transfer that attachment to us, eventually.

We had to keep working, and we had to have faith.

When I wrote *Orphan Song*, I wanted to dramatize everything about this necessity: the need for it, the difficulty of achieving it, the parental fear of its failure, the consequences of failure; the joys of little victories along the way. Also the differences in the way a child tests one parent vs. the other. With one it might just be: are you paying attention? Will you be patient? With the other, it might go straight to the heart of the matter: will you still love me even if I give you nothing back?

And I wanted to see what it was like for parents to discover working strategies in adoption for the first time—the first time in history.

This is an intensely emotional experience in our own modern times. When the stakes are life and death in the wilderness, I've discovered it becomes somewhat more harrowing. I'm sorry about that. Sorry, actors. Sorry, audience. Sorry!

There is a point in the play where the Neanderthal child cries out in the dark and a whole chorus of adult Neanderthal voices call back, frightening her. Gorse, her adoptive father—who is not Neanderthal but rather Early Modern Human—is happy at first that his daughter has suddenly nestled in to him for protection, fearful of her fellow "pipers" out there in the dark. It is a moment of weakness in him: after a night's contemplation, he comes around to the truth. Doing his best to explain and embrace his child's psychology, using only his limited 200-word vocabulary, he says,

"If Chicky fear they, Chicky fear all pipers; if Chicky fear all pipers, Chicky fear to live: Chicky fear Chicky."

(If the child is afraid of those Neanderthals out there in the dark, she will be afraid of all Neanderthals; if she is afraid of all Neanderthals, she will be afraid to live: She will be afraid of her own self.)

For me there is a straight line going back from writing this line to hearing my daughter's reaction to the assertion in the Little Gorilla book that everybody still loved him: "No." Parents have to find a way to turn that "no" into a "yes."

Two years after reading the story of the Little Gorilla, I was taking LRD in a wagon to daycare and she spotted a small dead rat on the sidewalk. It was curled up like it could have been sleeping. She saw it first, before I had the chance to prevent it, and said, "Look, a mouse!" I hastened her along.

And then, when we were about halfway to our destination, she said, "Daddy, I want to tell you something."

So I stopped the wagon, whose wheels are too loud to carry on a conversation while moving, and she said, very seriously and earnestly, "That mouse lost his family and he's all alone so maybe we should bring him inside our house and give him a home and a bed and feed him and make him part of our family. We should look after him and make him part of our family."

She had worked it all out in the two blocks between the dead rat and our pause on the sidewalk, and she was gazing up at me with big serious eyes.

This was a moment of pure joy for me. Don't get me wrong: the story wasn't over. Struggles go on. Feelings of abandonment resurface. Questions reassert themselves and must always be respected and addressed honestly.

But it's also true, as it was in this moment, that when adopted children have had their needs met—including a parental openness to a relationship with those who they once thought had abandoned them—they will come to have love for themselves, and empathy for anyone or anything whom they recognize as being in a situation that is similar to theirs.

Working with Puppet Master Kaitlin Morrow

I approached Kaitlin in 2019 when Richard was interviewing puppet designers. At the time Richard was talking to a guy with an impressive CV who was telling him that puppets could not run. There was a traumatized Neanderthal child at the centre of my play who 100% had to run. I got scared that Richard would hire this guy and slow down my traumatized child. In retrospect, I see that probably wouldn't have happened, but at the time, well, I kind of panicked.

Richard was also holding auditions for the puppeteer who would play the child. I had been pointed in Kaitlin's direction by Steve Fisher, who is one of our city's committed theatre-goers, attending alt comedy stages as much as the respectable, serious, adjective, adjective theatre. Surely a puppet-wielding comic who ran a company called Sex T-Rex would have no problem teaching a puppet how to run?

I wrote to Kaitlin, sent the script, begged K. to audition. Kaitlin went into that room with all those skills and came out with both the titular part AND the responsibility of building all the puppets in the play, as well as teaching all the other #OrphanSongTO actors how to operate them.

So then the nature of my panic changed. When Richard had asked me to read my own script to him, it had taken four months for me to figure out how to read the Chicky part right off the page. Now he had gone and given his lead actor a pig of a second job. And a third job, really. So I wrote to Kaitlin again, begging to meet up with me for bird-language coaching sessions, in exchange for bus tokens, vintage clothing, coloured stones, free plumbing and curtain-rod repair.

Our first meeting was a week before the pandemic was declared. We sat more than six feet apart. I don't think I was masked but I'm pretty sure I was wearing latex gloves, so my script did not catch COVID from me.

Then the spring 2020 production got shut down. Kaitlin had begun to build the puppets the previous summer, smuggling foam from Nova Scotia and also, I believe, ripping chunks out of sidewalk chesterfields on large item garbage days.

Those half-built puppets sat in a dark theatre for two years.

There was hope for the future, though, so we continued to meet for some birdy-lingo coaching, in exchange for window-washing, gummy bears, bicycle-chain oil, banjo lessons, sidewalk-chalk art. We met over that newfangled Zoom thing. We met in Christie Pits. It was cold sometimes. Sometimes it rained. Kaitlin learned those birdlike words well before rehearsals began.

Now, in rehearsal, when I watch Kaitlin Morrow work—both as Chicky and with the epic-makers, puppeteers Heather, Germaine, Phoebe, Kaitlyn, Ahmad, Daniel—I can see that, yes, Kaitlin can get that Chicky to run. But I am also seeing a stillness and grace that is reminiscent to me of the great French actor Jean-Louis Barrault in *Les Enfants du Paradis*, who used his body as a puppet. Kaitlin is like that too.

And the puppets are beautiful, though I should add that functionality comes first with them. Beauty comes later, as long as aesthetics don't get in the way of their capacity for expression. I love that. They're actors too, these puppets that Kaitlin has made. Part of the company too.

Sean Dixon

Production week note to Sophie Goulet

March 28th, 2022

Hey Sophie,

I just wanted to write and tell you how grateful I am that you've taken on this role and put so much of your heart and soul in it. I always thought this *Orphan Song* process would finally be the one where I would be able to return to full involvement through the rehearsal period, but it has turned out not to be the case. I've missed so many precious moments and I've been forced to listen in so much via remote and that all makes me sad that I don't get to know the company in the way that I used to, in the days before my life got so complicated, and so it becomes harder to properly express my deep gratitude and awe for the work you're doing and that you've done.

I always knew that Mo's was a hero's journey, but I had no idea how hard it all was for her. I've always felt that no matter how she might be feeling at any given moment, she is always thinking clearly and her ideas on what should be done are generally always the right ones, right up until she makes the mistake of leaving. And I guess I used to believe this strength of will and fierce intelligence made things easier for her to go through what she does, but I see now that it doesn't.

She's right about taking Chicky to the Neanderthals, way ahead of Gorse, who has to figure it out for himself. She's right about letting Chicky have the rabbit. She's right to take Chicky in in the first place, and make this family. She's even right about ensuring that Gran give her space. Chicky really does need to understand that Mo is the mother, and I think she's also right about Chicky loving Gran because it's easy and she doesn't need anything from her and they can be weak together. She might feel envious of Gran, but she knows that's all it is.

And when she decides to leave, I believe that mistake is partly Gorse's fault, because she has tried so hard to share her fears with him about Chicky's attachment, and he has failed to acknowledge those fears, leaving her feeling gas-lit and alone. I believe that if he had let himself be scared with her, she would never have had to leave. He's emotionally incapable of holding contradictory feelings. He's a bit of a coward that way and really lets her down.

But in living through her moment of weakness alone, she does reclaim her strength. That's a miracle, and I love watching you do that. I love it. Thank you. I had intended for this to be a brief note, sorry to go on.

S.

March 28th, 2022

Hi Sean,

What a lovely surprise to read your thoughtful and immensely generous email. Impeccably timed too and I was grateful to read your thoughts on Mo's journey. It's easy to get bogged down by the minutiae of beats and intentions within scenes, but to get such a clear and distilled overall picture is a gift, it brought everything into focus especially at this vulnerable crossroads, where our discoveries go public, so to speak.

Richard wisely says to trust the process. And so, to return the compliment: I thank you! You made it easy for me to trust. A character like Mo comes along once in a blue moon. You wrote the quintessential mother's journey and it is an honour to bring her to life. She is so richly layered and I'm grateful to be the first to give her a voice.

Looking forward to this week and the journey ahead! May it begin!

Mille mercis à toi, cher Sean.

Sincerely
Sophie

Understudying Chicky in Mandarin

When Phoebe Hu was asked to understudy the Chicky part, due to the risks of COVID, she consulted Kaitlin Morrow about Chicky's intonation and then rendered a more accurate score by using Mandarin characters that indicate pitch as much as pronunciation. I see fit to include this as the closing note to a play about language and communication.

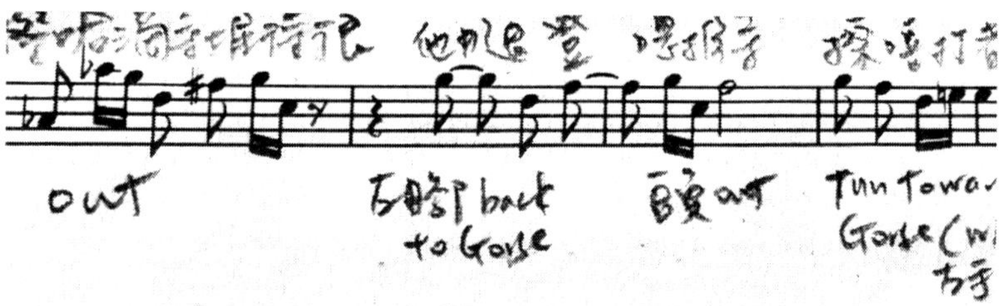